THE SEEDS OF HEAVEN

THE SEEDS OF HEAVEN

SERMONS ON THE
GOSPEL OF MATTHEW

Barbara Brown Taylor

WJK WESTMINSTER
JOHN KNOX PRESS
LOUISVILLE · KENTUCKY

Book design by Sharon Adams
Cover design by designpointinc.com

Published by Westminster John Knox Press
Louisville, Kentucky

This book is printed on acid-free paper that meets the American National Standards Institute Z39.48 standard. ∞

PRINTED IN THE UNITED STATES OF AMERICA

05 06 07 08 09 10 11 12 13—10 9 8 7 6 5 4 3

Library of Congress Cataloging-in-Publication Data

Taylor, Barbara Brown.
    The seeds of heaven : sermons on the Gospel of Matthew / Barbara Brown Taylor.—1st ed.
      p. cm.
  ISBN 0-664-22886-0 (alk. paper)
  1. Bible. N.T. Matthew—Sermons.   2. Episcopal Church—Sermons.   3. Sermons, American.   I. Title.
  BS2575.54.T39 2004
  252'.0373—dc22   2004050881

Contents

Preface to the New Edition

As a preacher, I have always envied poets. They do not have to come up with a new poem every week. They do not even have to say their poems out loud if they do not want to, but if they decide to do that then there is no shame in pulling out a sheaf of their old poems and reading some of their favorites. If they are published poets, then people may even ask them to read certain poems, and those same people are not disappointed when the poet says exactly what is printed on the page.

Preaching is not like that. Most people expect at least one new sermon from their preacher every week, and they tend to talk badly about those who work from sheaves of their old sermons. While some preachers may be forgiven for taking printed sermons into the pulpit, they are seldom forgiven for reading them. I can think of many reasons why this might be so, but the most obvious difference between a poem and a sermon is that a sermon is not about capturing the truth of life in words on a page. It is about bringing the truth in words on a page to life.

The best sermons are not essays but events. You have to be there, taking your part in the three-way encounter between a sacred text, a preacher, and a congregation. If you are not there, then you cannot know how a thundercloud passing suddenly overhead made all the windows in the church go dark just as the preacher got to the part about Jesus yelling Lazarus out of his tomb. If you are not there, then you have no idea whether the preacher embodied the good news she was proclaiming or whether her body language canceled it all out. In some cases, a printed sermon is no more than a rumor of what the sermon was really about.

Sometimes you cannot be there, of course. Sometimes you are sick, out of town, or estranged. Sometimes you cannot find a church anywhere near where you live that lets people wonder the sorts of things that you wonder about or asks people the kinds of questions that you want to be asked. In cases like these, a book of printed sermons can come in handy, if only to remind you that you are not as alone as you sometimes feel.

I even know a few preachers who need to be reminded of that. Some of them work so hard at reaching out to other people that they can end up with no one who knows how to care for them. They can use up all the holy words they have in a single day so that they have none left to pray with at night, much less to preach with on Sunday morning. In cases like these too, a book of printed sermons can come in handy, if only to kick-start a preacher's own creative process.

I am grateful to Jack Keller at Westminster John Knox Press for deciding to keep this volume in print. When most of the sermons in it were written, the pressing questions of the time included homelessness, AIDS, the widening gap between rich and poor, and the relevance of an ancient gospel to the busy lives of affluent, twentieth-century Christians. Fifteen years later the world has shifted on its axis. While none of the old questions have gone away, new ones have taken the lead. In the new millennium, what is the proper relationship between God and country? How should Christians live with those who are not Christian? Is the Bible the last word on human sexuality?

While you will not find answers to all of those questions in this book, you will find one preacher's attempt to speak of Christian faith in a way that honors both the holiness of Scripture and the holiness of real people's lives on earth. Three new sermons are included. Like the sermons prepared for the Protestant Hour, these too were composed for people whom I did not know—or at least I did not know their names, their professions, their family situations, or their congregational issues. Few guest preachers do. But I thought that I did know some other things about them, at least if they worried about the same things that I did.

I knew some of them doubted that their lives were as purposeful as God meant for them to be. I knew some of them wanted to be known as badly as they feared being known. I knew some of them woke up in the middle of the night and wondered how much longer they or the person they loved most in the world had left to live. Even when I am speaking to people whom I *do* know, these are the kinds of questions that keep me connected to my listeners. In the present case, I hope that they will keep me connected to my readers as well.

For once I get to act like a poet, presenting you with some old work in which I tried to capture a little of the truth of life in words on a page. The language is antique in some places, the theology dated. That makes you the preacher, whose job is to do more than read them. Your job is to find your own words for what matters most and then to give yourself fully to speaking them, so that anyone who looks at you can see God's own truth come to life.

Introduction to the 1990 Edition

The following sermons were all prepared for radio broadcast during the summer of 1990, when they were aired as the Episcopal Series of the Protestant Hour. For someone accustomed to preaching in a church full of rustling, responsive human beings, the exercise of preaching to a microphone was a strange one. Because I could not see those to whom I spoke, I had to imagine them: people of every description getting dressed in the morning, sitting at the kitchen table with a cup of coffee, driving the car, preparing a meal, filling a long afternoon, dozing in an easy chair after supper—whenever and wherever they might have decided to turn on their radios and let a stranger talk to them.

In order to speak to them I had to decide why they were listening, and I suspected that their reasons for enduring a sermon were the same as mine. I listen because I seek something: a sense of connection, a handle on mystery, an invitation to wonder. I listen because I hope to hear my own life described, my own fears addressed, and my own hopes fed. I listen for the same reason we all listen: to see if we can find God in the words and events that come our way each day.

A good preacher must first of all be a good listener. In the same way a child listens before learning to speak, a preacher cannot proclaim the word of God before listening to that word and wrestling with it until it has yielded its blessing. Only then does one dare to speak, building a fragile bridge of words between the ancient stories of the faith and the everyday stories of people's lives. It is hands-on work, which means that no preacher can present anyone with a bridge without having walked across it first. In this present collection, then, I invite you to walk with me into the spacious land of God's abiding presence with us all.

I want to thank Charles Long and Bob Horine of Forward Movement Publications for making these sermons available and Louis Schueddig and the Board of the Episcopal Radio-TV Foundation for inviting me to deliver them. I also want to thank my husband, Edward, who is a preacher's best friend. It is my hope that at least one of the words in this little book turns out to be God's word for you.

1

Exceeding Righteousness

Matthew 5:17–20

"Think not that I have come to abolish the law and the
prophets; I have come not to abolish them but to fulfil
them. For truly, I say to you, till heaven and earth pass
away, not an iota, not a dot, will pass from the law until all
is accomplished. Whoever then relaxes one of the least of
these commandments and teaches men so, shall be called
least in the kingdom of heaven; but he who does them and
teaches them shall be called great in the kingdom of
heaven. For I tell you, unless your righteousness exceeds
that of the scribes and Pharisees, you will never enter the
kingdom of heaven."

As the world grows smaller and followers of the world's religions
become literal next-door neighbors, the question of Christianity's relationship with those neighbors gains urgency. What
makes us like them? What makes us different? How do our
beliefs affect our neighborliness? While it may take us a while to
sort out our proximity to Hinduism or Taoism, our nearest
neighbor is and always has been Judaism. We share Scripture.
We share sacred sites. We share belief in the same God.
    Ironically, it is this very closeness that has made us enemies

over the years. We share one tradition that we interpret in different ways, because we do not share Jesus, or at least not as the Christ. His name divides Jews and Christians, the same way it divides the Bible in two. At issue is the Christian claim that Jesus is God incarnate, which for Judaism violates the first commandment. As I heard an Orthodox Jew say recently, "We believe in one God, period—no add-ons, no triumvirates."

Early belief in Jesus' divinity was based on many things. Even before his resurrection from the dead, there were miraculous feedings and healings. There were demonstrations of power over demons, storms, and even death itself. But just as important as those was the authority of his teaching, which sounded more like God to some of his listeners than what they were hearing from God's authorized spokespersons. From the Sermon on the Mount to his teaching in the temple, Jesus said things that made people swoon—both with fervor and with disbelief—because he taught things contrary to Torah.

Some scholars note that he never contradicted written tradition—only the oral tradition of the Pharisees—but the fact is that much of what he said went beyond or around what God had said through Moses. Whether the subject was the primacy of the family or the observance of the Sabbath, Jesus had some disturbing things to say—things that finally got him and his followers excluded from the synagogue. In spite of the way some Christians tell the story, this happened not because the synagogue was narrow-minded or corrupt but because the synagogue was faced with a vital choice: to remain loyal to the word of God through Moses, or to believe that God was speaking a new, improved word through Jesus. The majority of the Jews stuck with Moses, while the followers of Jesus went on to gain many converts among the Gentiles.

Until that turn toward the Gentiles, proper observance of Torah was not a burning issue in the church. In some places, Jewish Christians observed Sabbath on Saturday and met to break bread on Sunday. Many kept the same dietary laws that they had always kept. But with the inclusion of Gentiles in the church, the whole body of Torah came under fresh scrutiny. What was essential and what was not? What constituted the minimum requirements for following a Jewish messiah, and what could be jettisoned as relics of the past? The Christian question was how to remain obedient to God in a changed world. The New Testament is the record of not one but several answers to that question, all of them conditioned by the belief that the end was coming very soon.

The Gospel of Matthew is one answer, in which Jesus insists that he has come not to abolish Torah but to fulfill it. As fresh as Jesus' language sounded, as peculiar as the grammar of his life might seem, he did not intend to change one letter of the law, not one stroke of a letter, until all was accomplished. Jesus' argument was not with Torah but with those who did not follow Torah. He was as committed to the practice of righteousness as any scribe or Pharisee. Indeed, he was *more* committed: "For I tell you, unless your righteousness exceeds that of the scribes and Pharisees, you will never enter the kingdom of heaven."

This is a fascinating passage for all sorts of reasons. In the first place, it suggests that Jesus never intended to break with Judaism. If anything, he meant for his followers to become the most righteous Jews the world had ever seen. In the second place, the passage raises serious questions about Christianity's dismissal of Torah. With the possible exception of at least eight of the Ten Commandments, most Christians no longer observe the law of Moses. We regard Torah as fundamental to Judaism, not Christianity. Jews believe in Torah. We believe in Jesus, who freed us from the law. *Oh, really?* Not the Jesus of Matthew 5. The Jesus of Matthew 5 came to fulfill the law, not to abolish it.

Matthew could have coined the phrase "Judeo-Christian tradition." It summed up his understanding of Jesus as the Davidic messiah who had come to galvanize the people of God—not to choose a new people but to lead the already chosen people into the presence of God. No one was a greater champion of the Judeo-Christian tradition than Matthew.

So I am glad that he wasn't around a couple of hundred years later when the Christian Bible was put together. I am glad that he wasn't there to see his gospel set in a stack on the right (the

New Testament), while all of his beloved sources—Isaiah, Deuteronomy, Exodus, the Psalms—were set on the left (the Old Testament). It meant that his project had failed. It meant that there was no Judeo-Christian tradition after all, but a Jewish one that had given rise to a Christian one, which had turned out so differently that it required a division in the book. The Torah of Moses on one side, the teaching of Jesus on the other—not one covenant but two, an old one and a new one—with some nonnegotiable differences between the two.

On the whole, I think, Christians have overlooked those differences more than Jews have. We continue to use the term "Judeo-Christian" as if the one tradition flowed smoothly into the next. The only way we can do that, however, is by hijacking Judaism. Too many of us equate the law of Moses with the law of sin and death. We proclaim Jesus as the giver of a new law—the law of love—an easy yoke to replace the hard one. Through his own life and death he showed us what true love—true obedience—looked like, and by raising him from the dead God made him the Lord and paradigm for all life.

This popular telling overlooks the fact that there are more than thirteen million Jews in the world today who do not experience Torah as the law of sin and death. For them, Torah is the way of life, granted by God within a covenant of pure grace. It is the incarnation of God's love for humankind. It is the invitation to become holy as God is holy. Whether the yoke is easy or hard is not the point. The point is that it was given by God, as the crown and paradigm for all life.

So there is the choice, as Matthew's community faced it. Which was the true paradigm for life: Torah or Christ? When Jesus said "Follow me," instead of "Follow Torah," he cut a new fork in the road. Weighing the alternatives, the majority of Jews decided to go on following Torah, while those who followed Jesus believed that they had found in him the embodiment of Torah. They were the ones for whom "Judeo-Christian" made sense. For the rest, there was no hyphen between the two, but only a slash, as in "either/or."

As hard as Matthew worked to stress the continuities, there

were discontinuities as well. It helps to remember that there was no one Judaism in Jesus' day. There was the Judaism of the Galilee, which leaned toward the prophets, and the Judaism of Judea, which leaned toward the Temple. There was the Judaism of the Pharisees, who loved oral interpretation of Torah, and there was the Judaism of the Sadducees, who did not. There was the Judaism of Hillel, who taught that righteous Gentiles could enter the kingdom of heaven, and the Judaism of Shammai, who taught that they could not.

In this first-century stew of Jewishness, Jesus was one teacher among many with his own little-*t* torah—his own teaching about the capital-*T* teaching of Torah. On some points, his torah was very strict. He deepened the prohibition against murder to include anger, and the one against adultery to include lust. He narrowed the ground for divorce to unchastity, and said that remarriage after divorce was the same as sleeping around. On other points, his torah was very relaxed. As a Galilean, he was not scrupulous about some of the purity laws that chiefly concerned the priesthood in the Temple, and he was famously critical of the Pharisees' oral extension of the law.

When they questioned him about his disciples' poor handwashing techniques, they cited "the tradition of the elders"—for them, an oral tradition that was as old as Sinai and just as authoritative, but for other Jews, including Jesus, a strictly Pharisaic tradition that was not normative for everyone. There is nothing in the Torah of Moses about laypersons washing their hands before meals, Jesus pointed out to his critics, but the deeper question was one of authority that was not so easily settled.

On this point as well as others, Jesus was a fundamentalist. His teaching concerned what was written in Scripture, and he was skeptical of those who embellished it. But he was equally skeptical of those who gave every line of Scripture the same weight. Like other Jewish teachers of his time, he applied the hermeneutical principle of "light and heavy" to biblical commands. As far as he was concerned, the weightier matters of the law were justice and mercy and faith (Matt. 23:23). The lighter weight jots and tittles were not to be neglected, but neither were they allowed to get in the way. When obeying a light law got in the way of obeying a heavier law, then light yielded to heavy, so that God's will might be fulfilled.

So which was heavier, ritual cleanliness or open table fellowship? *Open table fellowship*, Jesus taught. Healing a withered hand or Sabbath observance? *Healing a withered hand*, Jesus taught. And that, of course, was where the trouble started. Who says what is light and what is heavy? By what authority are such judgments made? It was Jesus' answers to those questions, and not his violation of the law, that got him set outside the synagogue. After announcing his total loyalty to Torah in the middle of Matthew 5, Jesus went on to say—not once but six times—"You have heard that it was said . . . But I say to you . . ." If he had been offering an improvement on the teaching of other rabbis, then the formula might not have been shocking, but he was not. He was offering an improvement on the teaching of God through Moses. By what authority did he do such a thing?

"But I say to you," he said. He did it by his own authority, and when he was through there was a clear fork in the road. One way led to following Torah as it had been revealed by God to Moses. The other way led to following the teaching of this man, who claimed dominion over Torah itself—not *against* it, but *over* it—with God's own power to say what was heavy and what was light in the doing of God's will.

"Think not that I have come to abolish the law and the prophets; I have come not to abolish them but to fulfil them." Whether you attribute that pronouncement to Matthew or to Jesus, the truth of it lies in the word "fulfil," a word Matthew uses sixteen times in his Gospel to describe how Jesus brought Scripture to life. Jesus did this not by acting it out exactly as it was written on the page, but by acting like the one to whom all Scripture pointed. He did it by acting as God's son. For those who followed him, Jesus did not *recite* Torah; he *was* Torah. In his words and in his deeds, he was the living justice, mercy, and faith of God. Jesus did not *interpret* Torah; he *fulfilled* Torah in his flesh, and he promised those who followed him that they could fulfill it too. By example, he taught his followers that there would be times when this fulfillment would go further than the Torah on the page—that was the dangerous part. There would be times when the deepest possible obedience to God would look like disobedience to the keepers of the traditions of the elders, and no amount of arguing would settle the dispute about which commands were weighty and which were light.

This dangerous teaching of his—and our equally dangerous decision to believe it—still reverberates in our life together. It still fuels many of our church fights about how to remain obedient to God in a changed world. Do we follow the Torah on the page or the torah we are led to by the spirit of Jesus? By what authority does any of us challenge the tradition of our own Christian elders?

The same teaching also fuels the ongoing division between us and our first cousins the Jews. We share Scripture. We share sacred sites. We share belief in the same God, but we do not share Jesus, who taught a different torah from the Torah of Moses. For Jews, it is too light. For Christians, it is weighty— not the abolition of the law and the prophets but the fulfillment of them, in a life and death that lifted Torah off the page.

While we honor the commitments that divide us—both in the church and between church and synagogue—it would be good to remember that we share one more thing, and that is a call to exceeding righteousness. "For I tell you, unless your righteousness exceeds that of the scribes and Pharisees, you will never enter the kingdom of heaven."

In the best of both our traditions, this righteousness has never been a matter of following rules but of honoring relationships—with aliens as well as kin, with enemies as well as allies. The Torah of Moses and the torah of Jesus both agree on that. When we honor our neighbors—when we love them as ourselves—then, and only then, are we ready to discover what the law, the prophets, and the gospel are all about.

2

The Marginal Messiah

Matthew 11:2–11

Now when John heard in prison about the deeds of the Christ, he sent word by his disciples and said to him, "Are you he who is to come, or shall we look for another?" And Jesus answered them, "Go and tell John what you hear and see: the blind receive their sight and the lame walk, lepers are cleansed and the deaf hear, and the dead are raised up, and the poor have good news preached to them. And blessed is he who takes no offense at me."

As they went away, Jesus began to speak to the crowds concerning John: "What did you go out into the wilderness to behold? A reed shaken by the wind? Why then did you go out? To see a man clothed in soft raiment? Behold, those who wear soft raiment are in kings' houses. Why then did you go out? To see a prophet? Yes, I tell you, and more than a prophet. This is he of whom it is written, 'Behold, I send my messenger before thy face, who shall prepare thy way before thee.' Truly, I say to you, among those born of women there has risen no one greater than John the Baptist; yet he who is least in the kingdom of heaven is greater than he."

Most Christians are so familiar with the name "Jesus Christ" that it is easy to forget what a hard-won combination that was at first. Based on evidence that can be found in the New Testament, there were at least two early candidates for the job of Christ: Jesus the carpenter's son and John the Baptist, whom many believed to be the *true* Messiah of God. According to Luke, John's birth was also a miraculous one announced by the angel Gabriel. John was furthermore descended from priests on both his mother's and his father's sides, which meant that he wasted no time at all as a woodworker's apprentice. John was an evangelist from the word go.

While Jesus sat down to fancy suppers in town with people who drank too much and laughed too loud, John lived an austere life in the wilderness with his equally austere disciples. If he found something to eat, he ate. If he didn't, he didn't. He avoided alcohol altogether, the same way he avoided anything that might soften the sharpness of his focus on God.

Everything about John set him apart as a holy man: his way of life, his clothing, and above all his message. No one had heard anything like it in five hundred years. Ever since the time of Ezra and Nehemiah, the land of Israel had been passed from one superpower to another—from Greece to Egypt to Syria to Rome. The promised land had become a tarnished trophy handed from one empire to the next. The chosen people had become a conquered people, whose value lay chiefly in their ability to pay taxes. What was missing in all of this was any reaction from God. *Hello? Is anybody there?*

Where were the prophets who had once spoken for God to the people? Where was Nathan, opening King David's heart to the full impact of his affair with Bathsheba? Where was Elijah, calling down fire from heaven so that no one who saw it could doubt the power of God? Where was Amos, shouting himself hoarse about God's disgust with Israel's obscene wealth and empty religion?

Those voices had been missing in Israel for a long time when John the Baptist appeared in the wilderness sounding like God's own air raid siren. Finally, someone was speaking God's language again—talking about sin instead of profit, about repentance instead of compromise. John was not interested in helping people become more productive members of society.

He wanted them poised to enter God's kingdom, and he was happy to condemn anyone who stood in their way.

John let King Herod have it for being an all-around evil man. He let the Pharisees and Sadducees have it for teaching religiousness instead of righteousness. He promised everyone that God was coming with a sharpened axe in one hand and a flaming torch in the other, to clean up a world that had become impassable with dead wood.

John's gospel was an invigorating one that won him a lot of converts. Then John met Jesus, and things moved into high gear. Finally, it looked as if things were getting off the ground. Finally, God had sent the chosen one. Surely it would not be long before the Messiah established justice on the earth.

At least that was the hope, right there at the beginning. Then Herod's soldiers came with a warrant for John's arrest, and the man who had lived as far as he could from human corruption found himself caged in Herod's basement like a rat. The good news was that he was alone there. Jesus was still free, still hastening the kingdom, which may have been the only consolation John had.

Somehow or another, John kept up with what Jesus was doing. John's disciples found some way to get messages to him, and to carry his messages back. The early reports of Jesus' ministry were promising: healings, exorcisms, signs, and wonders. That was good. That would get people's attention for the big announcement. When Jesus finally declared God's judgment, that would give him the authority he needed.

Only the big announcement never came. While John sat muzzled in jail, all Jesus did was play doctor to some very marginal people—lepers, demoniacs, hemorrhaging women— even a Roman soldier's slave. What kind of witness was that to God's power? How was that going to help anyone know right from wrong?

It is not possible to know what John was thinking without resorting to fiction. We do not know what went on inside him while he sat in Herod's dungeon. We do know that Jesus never organized a picket outside the jail, or did anything else to try and get John released. We know that John's disciples came to

Jesus to question him about the laxity of his spiritual practice. And we know that John himself finally sent Jesus a message: "Are you he who is to come, or shall we look for another?"

It is hard to fathom the disappointment in that question. Was I wrong about you? I was sure wrong about something. If you know who you are, please just say so. If you are not the one, then we need to reopen the search process, and fast.

Only Jesus would not just say so. Instead, he turned John's disciples around so that they were not looking at Jesus but at some of the people who followed Jesus around. It was a gimpy, twitching group, sure enough, but they were more whole than they had ever been in their lives. They knew they were the lucky ones, too. There were plenty of blind people who were still blind, and plenty of dead people who were still dead. Jesus could not get around to everyone, but he had gotten around to them, and there was not one doubt in their minds who he really was.

"Go and tell John what you hear and see," Jesus said to John's disciples. "The blind receive their sight and the lame walk, lepers are cleansed and the deaf hear, and the dead are raised up, and the poor have good news preached to them. And blessed is he who takes no offense at me."

It was Isaiah's prophecy come to life—not the part John had been focused on, about God coming with vengeance, with terrible recompense—but the other part, about the lame leaping like deer and the tongue of the speechless singing for joy. As a loving P.S. to the one who had baptized him, Jesus added a new beatitude at the end. *And blessed is John for handling his disappointment in me.*

John had wanted a tidal wave of a Messiah—someone who would be impossible to miss, who would make a clean sweep of things, who would witness to the omnipotent righteousness of God. What John got instead was a steady drip of mercy from a man named Jesus, in whom plenty of people saw no Messiah at all. As far as anyone knows, John died unconvinced. He died wondering who Jesus was and what kind of joke God had played on him, to have made him the messenger for such a languid savior.

I wish I could tell you that Jesus' own death and resurrection changed everything—that once word got out what God had done with him, everyone saw the light and turned toward it on the spot. I wish I could tell you that today everyone believes in him, that is, believes that he wedged his body in the door between heaven and earth, and that through him God is at work in this world right now, bringing in the kingdom with power and great might.

You believe that, don't you? Maybe not everyone believes it, but at least you do. Don't you?

If you have one doubt in your mind, then I will tell you the truth. Sometimes I would give anything for one fireball from heaven, for one blast of raw power from a tidal wave God who would sweep my and everyone else's doubts away forever. But that is not what I have. What I have instead is a steady drip of mercy from the followers of a man named Jesus, who is still playing doctor to a lot of marginal people in this world.

Right after the awful floods in Honduras, I read about two paramedics who left their jobs in the United States and drove down to help pull bodies out of the mud. They did not speak the language. They did not know where they would stay once they got there. They did not even delude themselves that they were saving lives. They knew they were fishing for corpses, but they did it for the families. They thought it might help the living, to give them back their loved ones for burial.

In the same newspaper, I read about a hay farmer in the Midwest who had a lucky summer. He grew more fescue than he needed and was trying to decide what to do with it when he heard about an Indian reservation in the next state that had been hit hard by the drought. With no irrigation, the reservation's hay crop had been wiped out and its cows were starving. The farmer loaded up his truck and spent the rest of the week delivering tons of free hay to people who wondered what part of heaven he had dropped out of.

That reminded me of a woman from my hometown who somehow found her way to an orphanage in Russia, where she and her husband adopted a baby boy. As they walked through the gates of that place toward their rented car, she heard a little girl crying, "Dasvydonya, Mama. Dasvydonya, Papa." *Good-bye, Mama. Good-bye, Papa.* In her place, I would have focused on the one child I had helped instead of the hundreds I had not, but she could not do that. When she got home she started something called the StarFish Group, a nonprofit agency that is now dedicated to leading "unfound" parents in this country to their children in Russia.

I could go on and on. Drip. Drip. Drip. These are not big stories. They are small stories, in which only a few people at a time are saved. Meanwhile, there are many others who go on wondering if God has abandoned them. They listen to the bold claims of faith. They look at the modest returns. Who can blame them if they send their own message to Jesus: "Are you he who is to come, or shall we look for another?"

The only way I know how to answer them is to point out how stone is shaped by water. See that round hole there? Water did that. Drop by transparent, short-lived drop, water transforms rock as no tidal wave ever could. For reasons beyond our understanding, that is how the Messiah has decided to come for now—not all at once but steadily, drop by drop, for millennia. Every time someone lives as he lived by loving as he loved, another drop falls. For some people, it is not enough. For others, it is the way of life. And blessed are those who take no offense at him.

3

The Open Yoke

Matthew 11:25–30

At that time Jesus declared, "I thank thee, Father, Lord of heaven and earth, that thou hast hidden these things from the wise and understanding and revealed them to babes; yea, Father, for such was thy gracious will. All things have been delivered to me by my Father; and no one knows the Son except the Father, and no one knows the Father except the Son and any one to whom the Son chooses to reveal him. Come to me, all who labor and are heavy laden, and I will give you rest. Take my yoke upon you, and learn from me; for I am gentle and lowly in heart, and you will find rest for your souls. For my yoke is easy, and my burden is light."

These verses from the Gospel according to Matthew are the ones appointed for this fifth Sunday of Pentecost, that long season in the church year that stretches from the day of Pentecost in the spring until the first Sunday of Advent in November or December. It is a season during which we concentrate on sayings and stories from the life of Jesus in an effort to understand better our own stories and the story of the church. To help us in that task, the Episcopal Book of Common Prayer gives us something called the lectionary—a sort of assigned reading list for the church—one that leads us through a three-year cycle of readings from the Bible by appointing particular lessons for each Sunday of the year.

The beauty of the lectionary is that it leads us places we might not otherwise go. Certainly it includes many of our favorite passages, stories we learned as children and have returned to as adults, but it also includes passages that would be easy for us to overlook because they are unpleasant or hard to understand. By leading us to them, the lectionary makes sure that we do not read only the parts of the Bible we like and close the covers on all the rest.

The lectionary also gives us a sense of connection with Christians around the world, many of whom are reading and thinking about the same passages we are each week. Since the Episcopal Church follows a lectionary that coincides with those of many other denominations, there is a good chance that the Methodist, Presbyterian, Congregational, Lutheran, or Roman Catholic congregations in your own community are addressing the same verses of Scripture we are on any given Sunday morning.

For those reasons, my sermons these next twelve weeks will be based on the Gospel lessons appointed for each Sunday by the lectionary. One of the reasons it is a three-year lectionary is so we can spend a full year on each of the first three Gospels— one on Matthew, one on Mark, and one on Luke—with readings from the Fourth Gospel scattered throughout. This year is Matthew's year, which means that over the next three months we will attend to his version of Christ's life and ministry, a version that includes famous stories such as the feeding of the five thousand and Peter's walk across the water as well as the parables of the Sower and the Pearl of Great Price.

This morning's reading contains one of the great consolation passages of all time. "Come to me, all who labor and are heavy laden," Jesus says, "and I will give you rest." It is a passage you can find etched on tombstones or worked into stained glass windows or maybe even stitched in needlepoint and hung in the church parlor. My strongest memory of it dates back to my year as a hospital chaplain, when I conducted Sunday services in a tiny chapel on the ground floor of a big city hospital.

Every Sunday morning at ten my congregation of four, or five, or six would arrive: a man in pajamas pushing an IV pole, a patient from the psychiatric ward chaperoned by an orderly, the parents of a child who lay close to death from spinal meningitis up on the sixth floor. One by one they hauled their grief and misery into that little chapel where there was not much to see— just an electric organ, and the backs of one another's heads, and a simple pulpit made out of light oak with a few words carved on the front of it: "Come unto me, all ye who labor and are heavy laden, and I will refresh you."

It is a wonderful promise, a comforting promise to which many of us turn when our burdens seem impossible to bear, when our best efforts to cope with them have failed and we are close to collapse. It is a promise that offers hope of help, hope of a God who will lift the sweaty loads off our backs and replace them with a lighter yoke, lighter because it yokes us with one who is greater than we are, and with whose strong help we can bear any burden.

That is what the passage means to many of us today, but it meant something different when Jesus first said it. He had just finished a preaching mission to several Galilean cities, where his welcome had been less than warm. The people in those cities were smart and capable. In spite of Roman occupation, both their local economies and their religious institutions were still working. They were not looking for help from Jesus or anyone else, and whatever gifts he had hoped to give to them, they declined to take.

This Galilean mission was a failure, in other words, and in the passage at hand we hear Jesus' response to that failure. After heaping some powerful reproaches on those who did not welcome him, he thanks God for showing things to simple people that wise and understanding people cannot see. At least one reason why this is God's will, apparently, is so that no one gets human wisdom and understanding confused with divine revelation. Those who know God do not arrive at such knowledge by their own natural intelligence or capable efforts. They know God because God has chosen to be known.

Next Jesus offers to lighten the load of all who are carrying heavy burdens, some of which have presumably been laid on the shoulders of the simple people by the wise and understanding ones. In the first century, this burden might have been literal sticks and bricks, the increasing weight of Rome, or the more invisible load of any life's grief and fear. But since this is Matthew's Gospel, it is likely that Jesus meant religious burdens as well. By the time Matthew sat down to write, the first Jewish revolt had failed and the Temple was in ruins. With the Sadducees out of business and the Zealots in full retreat, the Pharisees were the only religious party left standing, with the future of Judaism in their hands. This placed them on a collision course with Jesus' party, and in many ways Matthew's Gospel is a record of their struggle.

In those days, the Jesus party was by far the smaller of the two. It was made up largely of simple people who were stung by the inhospitality of the wise and understanding people to whom they believed they belonged. Both parties shared the same Torah, the same prophets, the same devotion to the same God. Two millennia later, with their separation official and their numbers reversed, it is easy to cast the struggle between them as one between Jews and Christians, but in Jesus' day it was a struggle among his own people, no less bitter than those in some Christian circles today. At issue were not only who had authority to speak for God but also what those authorities said about the kind of yoke God placed on humankind.

Then, as now, some proposed weightier requirements than others. Then, as now, some placed more weight on their own view of those requirements than others. If you read the newspaper—or if you belong to a faith community yourself—then you know that such debate did not only happen once long ago in a land far away; it continues to happen right now, wherever religious people meet to decide what it means to know God. In this light, Matthew's Gospel is not about a struggle between two different religious traditions. It is about the struggle within one religious tradition over the requirements of faith.

Thanks to the apostle Paul and his gifted interpreter Martin Luther, most Christians identify this struggle as one between works and grace. In traditional telling, when Jesus offered his heavy-laden listeners a lighter yoke, he was offering them a religion of grace to replace the religion of works under which they were laboring. I confess with sorrow that I have preached that sermon myself. Offering my faith community the high ground while denigrating the competition, my reading was not true on many levels. It was not historically true. It was not theologically true. It was not even humanly true.

As best I can tell, the truth is that every human being who longs to know God lives with the tension between grace and works. On one hand, we long to believe that God comes to us as we are, utterly unimpressed by the tricks we do for love. On the other hand, we live in a world where those tricks often work really well, so that it is next to impossible to give up believing in them too. Follow us around for a day or two and you may discover what we believe most by how we act.

I may believe that I live by God's grace, but I act like a scout collecting merit badges. I have a list of things to do that is a mile long, and while there are a number of things on the list that I genuinely want to do, the majority of them are things I think I ought to do, that I should do, that I had better do or God will not love me anymore. I may believe that my life depends on God's grace, but I act like it depends on me and how many good deeds I can perform, as if every day were a talent show and God had nothing better to do than keep up with my score.

Do you know what I mean? Human beings have a perverse way of turning Jesus' easy yoke back into a hard one again, by driving ourselves to do, do, do more and whipping ourselves to be, be, be more when all God has ever asked is that we belong to him. That comes first; everything else follows that, but we so often get the order reversed. We think there are all kinds of requirements to be met first, all kinds of rules to follow, all kinds of burdens to bear, so that we are not yet free to belong to God. We are still loaded down, not only by our jobs and our families and all our other responsibilities but by something deeper down in us, something that keeps telling us we must do more, be better, try harder, prove ourselves worthy or we will never earn God's love. It is the most tiring work in the world, and it is never done.

One September a couple of years ago, I had more to do than any one person could do, and it was my own fault. I was not very good at saying no. I liked being needed and I liked being liked, and carrying a heavy load seemed like the best way to get to be both of those. Carrying it alone worked even better, because I did not have to share the rewards of my labor with anyone else. While I would not have admitted it at the time and I do not like admitting it now, I somehow had the idea that God expected more of me than of other people and that I could not let God down.

So I worked a couple of sixty-hour weeks in a row and told myself that I could rest as soon as I got it all done. I did not sleep well and my back began to hurt, but I pressed on, until one morning an unexpected thing happened: I could not get out of bed. The muscles in my back had gone on strike, and I could not move. First I panicked, and then I did all the things that religious people do when they do not like what life has dealt them. I pleaded with God, I bargained with God, I assured God that I had gotten the message, that I would slow down and stop playing superwoman if I could just get out of bed.

No deal. God would not play my game, so there I lay for the next week, my list of things to do gathering dust on the bureau, my appointment book lying neglected by the bed. At first it drove me crazy to look at them, but slowly, as the week wore on, they lost their power over me. I became more interested in watching how the sunlight moved across the ceiling as morning turned to afternoon. I slept a lot and read a lot and thought a lot about what really mattered in life and what did not. I visited with friends who came to call and spent more time with my family than I had in years.

It was an easy time that I remember now quite fondly. It was an easy yoke, but not one I would voluntarily have chosen. I thought that the way to find rest for my soul was to finish my list of things to do and present it to God like a full book of savings stamps, but as it turned out that was not the ticket at all. The way to find rest for our souls is simply to stop, to lay down our list of things to do and be, the heavy yokes we have designed for ourselves, and to accept the lighter ones God has made for us instead.

If you have traveled around the world or even if you have read *National Geographic* from time to time, you know that there are two basic kinds of yokes that can be used to bear burdens: single ones and shared ones. The single ones are very efficient. By placing a yoke across the shoulders and fitting buckets hung from poles on each side, human beings can carry almost as much as donkeys. They will tire easily and have to sit down to rest, and their shoulders will ache all the time—their backs may even give out—but still it is possible to move great loads from one place to another using a single creature under a single yoke.

A shared yoke works quite differently. It requires twice as many creatures for one thing, but if they are a well-matched pair they can work all day, because under a shared yoke one can rest a little while the other pulls. They can take turns bearing the brunt of the load; they can cover for each other without ever laying their burden down because their yoke is a shared one. They have company all day long, and when the day is done both may be tired but neither is exhausted, because they are a team.

Plenty of us labor under the illusion that our yokes are single ones, that we have got to go it alone, that the only way to please God is to load ourselves down with heavy requirements—good deeds, pure thoughts, blameless lives, perfect obedience—all those rules we make and break and make and break, while all the time Jesus is standing right there in front of us, half of a shared yoke across his own shoulders, the other half wide open and waiting for us, a yoke that requires no more than that we step into it and become part of a team.

"Come to me, all who labor and are heavy laden, and I will give you rest." No wonder those words have weathered the centuries so well; no wonder they are still music to our ears.

They assure us that those who please God are not those who can carry the heaviest loads alone but those who are willing to share their loads, who are willing to share their yokes by entering into relationship with the one whose invitation is a standing one. "Take my yoke upon you, and learn from me; for I am gentle and lowly in heart, and you will find rest for your souls. For my yoke is easy, and my burden is light."

4

The Extravagant Sower

Matthew 13:1–9, 18–23

That same day Jesus went out of the house and sat beside the sea. And great crowds gathered about him, so that he got into a boat and sat there; and the whole crowd stood on the beach. And he told them many things in parables, saying: "A sower went out to sow. And as he sowed, some seeds fell along the path, and the birds came and devoured them. Other seeds fell on rocky ground, where they had not much soil, and immediately they sprang up, since they had no depth of soil, but when the sun rose they were scorched; and since they had no root they withered away. Other seeds fell upon thorns, and the thorns grew up and choked them. Other seeds fell on good soil and brought forth grain, some a hundredfold, some sixty, some thirty. He who has ears, let him hear . . .

"Hear then the parable of the sower. When anyone hears the word of the kingdom and does not understand it, the evil one comes and snatches away what is sown in his heart; this is what was sown along the path. As for what was sown on rocky ground, this is he who hears the word and immediately receives it with joy; yet he has no root in himself, but endures for a while, and when tribulation or persecution arises on account of the word, immediately he falls away. As for what was sown among thorns, this is he

who hears the word, but the cares of the world and the
delight in riches choke the word, and it proves unfruitful.
As for what was sown on good soil, this is he who hears the
word and understands it; he indeed bears fruit, and yields,
in one case a hundredfold, in another sixty, and in another
thirty."

The parable of the Sower is one of seven such stories in the
thirteenth chapter of Matthew. As different as they can be, they
are all parables of the kingdom. "The kingdom of heaven is like
a mustard seed," Jesus tells the crowds on the shore of the lake,
"like treasure lying buried in a field, like yeast, like a pearl of
great price, like a net let down in the sea." He is teaching from
the prow of a boat because it is the only place he can find to sit;
so many have come to hear him, to learn from him, to touch
and be touched by him that there is no space left in their midst.
So he steps into a boat and speaks to them across the water, his
figure swaying a little with each lift of the waves, his words as
full of life and as hard to hold as a handful of lake.

If the crowds have come for lectures in practical theology
that day, then they are disappointed; what they get instead are
more like dreams or poems, in which images of God's kingdom
are passed before them—as familiar as the crops in their own
fields and the loaves in their own kitchens—but with a strange
new twist. Jesus seems to be saying that these ordinary things
have something important to do with God's purpose for them,
that these things they handle every day of their lives are vessels
of some sort, illustrations of some truth that seems clear to
them one moment and hidden the next—like seed flung to the
four winds, like buried treasure, like a net let down to the
depths of the sea.

Jesus' parables conceal his meaning even as they reveal it,
and some say it was how he stayed out of jail. He could have
been arrested for talking heresy and treason, after all, but for
talking about seeds and thorns, good soil and bad? Not likely.

By speaking in parables, Jesus could get his message across
without saying it directly, so that his followers nodded and
smiled while his critics scratched their bewildered heads. He

speaks in parables, he says, so that only certain kinds of listeners can hear him—those who listen less with their minds than with their hearts.

The parable of the Sower is a familiar one to most of us. In it, a sower casts seed on four kinds of ground: first, the packed ground of a footpath, then ground that is full of rocks, then ground that is thick with thorns, and finally good fertile ground. Depending on where they land, the seeds are eaten by birds, or spring up quickly and then wither away, or get choked by thorns, while some of them—roughly a quarter of them—take root in good soil.

I remember seeing this parable acted out in the stage production of "Godspell," a good-humored play based on the Gospel according to Matthew. Four rambunctious actors dressed like clowns played the seeds, each of them meeting a different fate. The seed that was cast on the path no sooner hit the ground than other actors making crow noises flapped down and pecked him to death. The seed that was cast on rocky ground came to life with a bang, waving her arms around and dancing in place, but then an actor carrying a big yellow cardboard sun stood over her until she grew limp and crumpled to the stage.

The seed that was cast among thorns barely had time to get to his knees before he was surrounded by prickly looking characters who got their hands around his neck and choked him. He was a ham, who made a lot of noise and took a long time biting the dust, but finally he too was dead. Then there was the seed that was cast on good soil, who came gracefully to life and stayed alive, bowing as both the audience and her fellow actors gave her a round of applause.

Watching all of that, I had the same response I always do to this parable: I started worrying about what kind of ground I was on with God. I started worrying about how many birds were in my field, how many rocks, how many thorns. I started worrying about how I could clean them all up, how I could turn myself into a well-tilled, well-weeded, well-fertilized field for the sowing of God's word. I started worrying about how the odds were three to one against me—those are the odds in the parable, after all—and I began thinking about how I could beat the odds, or at least improve on them, by cleaning up my act.

That is my usual response to this parable. I hear it as a challenge to be different, as a call to improve my life, so that if the same parable were ever told about me it would have a happier ending, with all of the seed falling on rich, fertile soil. But there is something wrong with that reading of the parable, because if that is what it is about, then it should be called the parable of the different kinds of ground.

Instead, it has been known for centuries as the parable of the Sower, which means that there is a chance, just a chance, that we have got it all backwards. We hear the story and think it is a story about us, but what if we are wrong? What if it is not about us at all but about the sower? What if it is not about our own successes and failures and birds and rocks and thorns but about the extravagance of a sower who does not seem to be fazed by such concerns, who flings seed everywhere, wastes it with holy abandon, who feeds the birds, whistles at the rocks, picks his way through the thorns, shouts hallelujah at the good soil and just keeps on sowing, confident that there is enough seed to go around, that there is plenty, and that when the harvest comes at last it will fill every barn in the neighborhood to the rafters?

If this is really the parable of the Sower and not the parable of the different kinds of ground, then it begins to sound quite new. The focus is not on us and our shortfalls but on the generosity of our maker, the prolific sower who does not obsess about the condition of the fields, who is not stingy with the seed but who casts it everywhere, on good soil and bad, who is not cautious or judgmental or even very practical, but who seems willing to keep reaching into his seed bag for all eternity, covering the whole creation with the fertile seed of his truth.

We would not do it that way, of course. If we were in charge, we would devise a more efficient operation, a neater, cleaner, more productive one that did not waste seed on birds and rocks and thorns, but concentrated only on the good soil and what we could make it do. But if this is the parable of the *sower*, then Jesus seems to be suggesting that there is another way to go about things, a way that is less concerned with productivity than with plenitude.

Not long ago, a friend and I made a pilgrimage to Howard Finster's Paradise Garden in Pennville, Georgia, about an hour and a half up the road from where I live. If you read *People* magazine or keep up with the world of art, then you know that Howard Finster is a folk artist of some repute, a seventy-three-year-old visionary who has painted close to ten thousand of his visions—on plywood, broken mirrors, Nehi soda bottles, canned-ham tins, old refrigerators, mailboxes, Delta airline plates, high-topped sneakers, and even an old Cadillac that is rusting in his garage.

Finster started out as a Baptist preacher and served eight or nine churches in rural Georgia and Alabama before he became disillusioned in the early 1970s. After preaching 4,625 sermons, he says, after presiding at more than 400 funerals and 200 weddings, he conducted a survey at his church and found out that no one remembered anything he had said. So he retired from preaching and began fixing things instead—televisions and bicycles, mainly—until 1976, when an inner voice from God told him to paint sacred art. "I cain't," Finster told the voice, "I'm no professional."

"How do you know you cain't?" the voice demanded, and Finster's career as an artist began. His work is both beautiful and bizarre, but equally fascinating is his three-acre Paradise Garden, under construction for the past twenty years, which Finster says he has "consecrated to all the inventions of nature and man."

I have been there twice and have only begun to take it all in, but if you follow the walkways that are embedded with old watches, gears, jewelry, marbles, and pottery shards, you cannot miss the twenty-foot tower fashioned from old bicycles, crowned with a cross made out of two lawn mower handles, or the two-ton concrete shoe, or the pump house made from Coca-Cola bottles. There is an aquarium that holds the bones of a three-legged chicken, a shed full of old sewing machines, a six-foot mound of serpents sculpted from poured cement; there are bubble gum machines, bunk bed springs, empty picture frames, and flights of stairs that lead nowhere.

You might think nature would be offended by such a display, but it is not so. The whole garden is covered by a canopy of muscadine vines heavy with ripening fruit; there are blueberry bushes and blackberry vines and day lilies blooming among the clutter; there are hens laying eggs and bees making honey and tadpoles turning into frogs. It is, quite simply, the most gorgeous pile of garbage I have ever seen.

The hand-painted sign on Finster's front porch sums it up, at least for him, and this is what it says: "I took the pieces you threw away, and put them together night and day; washed by rain, dried by sun, a million pieces all in one." The man is excessive, to say the least. Although he reckons that he records only about one out of a hundred of his visions, still he is extravagant; he is outrageous; there is not a moderate bone in his body. I look at his garden and I want to weed, neaten, organize; I want to ask him what everything means and post helpful signs for those who come after me. But Finster has already posted signs of his own. "I built this park of broken pieces to try to mend a broken world," says one, while another reads, "It's watermelon time; get your knife; eat, shout and shine."

"What I do talks," he says in a recent interview. "I figure when I'm deceased my work will be talking same as if I was here. Jesus used things that was familiar to people to get the subject over to them." Howard Finster pauses. "God's message is getting around."

Once upon a time a sower went out to sow. And as he sowed, some seeds fell along the path, and the birds came along and devoured them. So he put his seed pouch down and spent the next hour or so stringing aluminum foil all around his field. He put up a fake owl he ordered from a garden catalog and, as an afterthought, he hung a couple of traps for the Japanese beetles.

Then he returned to his sowing, but he noticed some of the seeds were falling on rocky ground, so he put his seed pouch down again and went to fetch his wheelbarrow and shovel. A couple of hours later he had dug up the rocks and was trying to think of something useful he could do with them when he remembered his sowing and got back to it, but as soon as he did he ran right into a briar patch that was sure to strangle his little seedlings. So he put his pouch down again and looked every-where for the weed poison but finally decided just to pull the thorns up by hand, which meant that he had to go back inside and look everywhere for his gloves.

Now by the time he had the briars cleared it was getting dark, so the sower picked up his pouch and his tools and decided to call it a day. That night he fell asleep in his chair reading a seed catalog, and when he woke the next morning he walked out into his field and found a big crow sitting on his fake owl. He found rocks he had not found the day before and he found new little leaves on the roots of the briars that had broken off in his hands. The sower considered all of this, push-ing his cap back on his head, and then he did a strange thing: He began to laugh, just a chuckle at first and then a full-fledged guffaw that turned into a wheeze at the end when his wind ran out.

Still laughing and wheezing he went after his seed pouch and began flinging seeds everywhere: into the roots of trees, onto the roof of his house, across all his fences and into his neigh-bors' fields. He shook seeds at his cows and offered a handful to the dog; he even tossed a fistful into the creek, thinking they might take root downstream somewhere. The more he sowed, the more he seemed to have. None of it made any sense to him, but for once that did not seem to matter, and he had to admit that he had never been happier in all his life.

Let those who have ears to hear, hear.

5

Learning to Live with Weeds

Matthew 13:24–30, 36–43

Another parable he put before them, saying, "The kingdom of heaven may be compared to a man who sowed good seed in his field; but while men were sleeping, his enemy came and sowed weeds among the wheat, and went away. So when the plants came up and bore grain, then the weeds appeared also. And the servants of the householder came and said to him, 'Sir, did you not sow good seed in your field? How then has it weeds?' He said to them, 'An enemy has done this.' The servants said to him, 'Then do you want us to go and gather them?' But he said, 'No; lest in gathering the weeds you root up the wheat along with them. Let both grow together until the harvest; and at harvest time I will tell the reapers, Gather the weeds first and bind them in bundles to be burned, but gather the wheat into my barn'" . . .

Then he left the crowds and went into the house. And his disciples came to him, saying, "Explain to us the parable of the weeds of the field." He answered, "He who sows the good seed is the Son of man; the field is the world, and the good seed means the sons of the kingdom; the weeds are the sons of the evil one, and the enemy who sowed them is the devil; the harvest is the close of the age, and the reapers are angels. Just as the weeds are gathered and burned with fire, so will it be at the close of the age. The Son of man will send his angels, and they will gather out of his kingdom all causes of sin and all evildoers, and throw them into the furnace of fire; there men will weep and gnash their teeth. Then the righteous will shine like the sun in the kingdom of their Father. He who has ears, let him hear."

For two weeks now we have been reading stories from the Gospel according to Matthew, and just lately his version of our Lord's parables about the kingdom of heaven. It is like seed sown on different kinds of ground, he says, like a man who sowed good seed in his field, or—tune in next week—like a grain of mustard seed. No one can say for sure how accurate a reporter Matthew is, but one thing is certain: He warms up to any parable that has to do with judgment.

Of all the Gospel writers, he is the only one who waxes eloquent about the end of the world, the only one who mentions a furnace of fire where there will be weeping and gnashing of teeth. His is the only Gospel that contains the wise and foolish virgins, or the division of the sheep from the goats, or today's parable about the wheat and the weeds. Of all the Gospel writers, it is Matthew who most wants a clear-cut creation, in which things are black or white, good or bad, in which people are faithful or wicked, blessed or cursed.

It is something he has in common with the early Christians to whom today's parable is addressed, or at least to them among others. One version of the parable is told to the crowds, according to Matthew, and an annotated version to the disciples themselves—again, Matthew's discrimination between insiders and outsiders, between those with ears to hear and those without. To the insiders, the message is clear: Never mind that there seem to be a lot of weeds in the world right now. Hang in there, be patient. When the last day comes the wheat will be vindicated, while the weeds will go up in smoke.

It may have been a comforting message at the time, but in these latter days it tends to have the opposite effect. Matthew may have been clear that there are only two kinds of people in the world—the wheat and the weeds—but it is a clarity that escapes most of us, we who have encountered both kinds in ourselves, and in our neighbors, and in the world. Most of our fields are full of mixed plantings, or worse. Sometimes I think that if I examined mine closely I would not find wheat *or* weeds anymore. They have grown together for so long that a hybrid would be more likely, a mongrel seed that is neither one nor the other. So the business about gathering and burning the weeds tends to make me a little nervous, and the burning question is: Which am I? Wheat or weed? Blessed or cursed?

The lovely thing about parables is that they rarely answer such questions, or at least not directly. However much we want to read them like Morse code, they behave more like dreams or poems instead, delivering their meaning in images that talk more to our hearts than to our heads. Parables are mysterious, and their mystery has everything to do with their longevity. Left alone, they teach us something different every time we hear them, speaking across great distances of time and place and understanding.

But according to Matthew, Jesus does *not* leave today's parable alone. According to Matthew, he takes his disciples aside and gives them the key: He is the sower, the field is the world, the weeds belong to the devil, the wheat to the kingdom of God. Everything equals something else with nothing left over, and when you hear it all laid out like that you wonder why he did not just *say* so in the first place. Some scholars say it is how he avoided arrest; some say it was how he winnowed his listeners. Others say he never explained his parables at all, but that those who recorded his words could not stand their ambiguity, and took the liberty of making a few additions so that no one who heard them later could misunderstand.

Not that it matters much, except to remind us how much we love explanations, which are after all so much easier than mysteries. A parable washes over you like a wave full of life and light, but an explanation—well, an explanation lets you know where you stand. It gives you something to work with, a tool with which to improve yourself and the condition of the world in general. An explanation gives you something to put on the

church marquee for Sunday morning, like the one on the
Methodist Church where I live: "Don't Let the Weeds Take
Over," it reads this week, a message that the servants in today's
parable take to heart.

They are so eager to please. They see something awry in
their boss's best field and offer to fix it. "Do you want us to go
and gather the weeds?" they ask, wanting to be faithful servants,
to be counted among the sheep, to be counted good. The weeds
they are after are darnel—tares, if your Bible is the King James
Version, or *Lolium temulentum*, if you know your weeds—a
plant related to wheat, that looks like wheat, that hides out in
wheat but that is poisonous in the end, causing blindness and
even death if too many of its small black seeds turn up in the
bread dough.

Palestinian farmers learned to deal with it early, uprooting
the darnel once or twice before harvest so that they did not
have to separate the seeds by hand. To let the wheat and the
darnel grow together posed an unnecessary risk, but one that
this morning's sower seems willing to take. He is eccentric,
even by ancient standards—reluctant to let his servants weed
his field for fear they will uproot the wheat, certain that an
enemy is responsible for the problem in the first place. By
modern standards he seems a little paranoid—I mean, how
many of us assume that the weeds in our yards are the work of
our enemies?

But my husband, Edward, assures me that the biblical
account has merit, that he in fact took part in a similar raid
upon good seed while he was an undergraduate at Georgia
Tech, where late one night he and his fraternity brothers sowed
kudzu seeds in their rivals' freshly cultivated lawn and waited
with glee for the weed to take over the unsuspecting zoysia.

If you are not a southerner, I should explain that kudzu is our
version of darnel, except that it does not look anything like
wheat. It looks instead like whatever it has recently consumed,
which may include groves of pecan trees, rows of telephone
poles, or entire houses. It is possible, while touring the South,
to believe that you are driving through Appalachian foothills
when you are in fact viewing small mountains of kudzu that

have taken over everything in its path. Kudzu grows as much as twelve inches in a twenty-four-hour period, up to fifty feet in a single season, which explains its reputation as "the vine that ate the South."

"If you are going to plant kudzu," the saying goes, "drop it and run," but no one down south plants kudzu, although there are plenty of us who would like to get our hands on the scoundrel who did. Just for the record, kudzu was brought to this country to decorate the Japanese pavilion at the Philadelphia Centennial Exposition of 1876. An exotic import, it became popular as a shade plant, a hay and forage crop, and as the God-given solution to erosion after the Great Depression.

Kudzu soon became the darling of the Soil Conservation Service. Between 1935 and 1942, government nurseries produced 84 million kudzu seedlings and planted them wherever they would grow. By 1943, the Kudzu Club of America had 20,000 members, and southern belles competed for the coveted title of Kudzu Queen. Kudzu replaced cotton as the crop of the future, but the vine's chief virtue—its magnificent rate of growth—soon turned out to be its fatal flaw. Fruit growers began to complain that kudzu was choking their orchards, farmers reported that it broke their baling machines, and railroad engineers accused it of causing trains to slip off their tracks.

It was not long before the kudzu nurseries shut down, the Kudzu Club was disbanded, and the United States Department of Agriculture demoted kudzu to weed status, a weed being defined as "a plant that does more harm than good." Today kudzu is just a nuisance, an eyesore and a constant reminder that the rain falls on the just and the unjust alike.

Sometimes it is mighty hard to tell the difference between a good plant and a bad one, especially when it can act both ways. I suppose we have all had the experience of uprooting the raspberries by mistake or protecting something interesting that turns out to be a thistle. I don't know what makes us think we are any smarter about ourselves or about the other people in our lives. We are so quick to judge, as if we were sure we knew the difference between wheat and weeds, good seed and bad, but that is seldom the case. Turn us loose with our machetes and there is no telling what we will chop down and what we will spare. Meaning to be good servants, we go out to do battle with the weeds and end up standing in a pile of wheat.

Or else we do not, because we have the good sense to listen to the sower, whose orders sound foolhardy if not downright dangerous. Leave the weeds and the wheat alone; let them both grow together, he says, letting us know that he does not share our appetite for a pure crop, a neat field, an efficient operation; letting us know that growth interests him more than perfection and that he is willing to risk fat weeds for fat wheat. When we try to help him out a little, to improve on his plan, he lets us know that our timing is off, not to mention our judgment, and that he does, after all, own the field.

Hear another parable of the wheat and the weeds. One afternoon in the middle of the growing season, a bunch of farmhands decided to surprise their boss and weed his favorite wheat field. No sooner had they begun to work, however, than they began to argue—first about which of the wheat-looking things were weeds and then about the rest of the weeds. Did the Queen Anne's lace pose a real threat to the wheat, or could it stay for decoration? And the blackberries? They would be ripe in just a week or two, but they were, after all, weeds—or were they? And the honeysuckle—it seemed a shame to pull up anything that smelled so sweet.

About the time they had gotten around to debating the purple asters, the boss showed up and ordered them out of his field. Dejected, they did as they were told. Back at the barn he took their machetes away from them, poured them some lemonade, and made them sit down where they could watch the way the light moved across the field. At first, all they could see were the weeds and what a messy field it was, what a discredit to them and their profession, but as the summer wore on they marveled at the profusion of growth—tall wheat surrounded by tall goldenrod, ragweed, and brown-eyed Susans. The tares and the poison ivy flourished alongside the Cherokee roses and the milkweed, and it *was* a mess, but a glorious mess, and when it had all bloomed and ripened and gone to seed the reapers came.

Carefully, gently, expertly, they gathered the wheat and made the rest into bricks for the oven where the bread was baked. And the fire that the weeds made was excellent, and the flour that the wheat made was excellent, and when the harvest was over the owner called them all together—the farmhands, the reapers, and all the neighbors—and broke bread with them, bread that was the final distillation of that whole messy, gorgeous, mixed-up field, and they all agreed that it was like no bread any of them had ever tasted before and that it was very, very good. Let those who have ears to hear, hear.

6

The Seeds of Heaven

Matthew 13:31–33, 44–49

Another parable Jesus put before them, saying, "The kingdom of heaven is like a grain of mustard seed which a man took and sowed in his field; it is the smallest of all seeds, but when it has grown it is the greatest of shrubs and becomes a tree, so that the birds of the air come and make nests in its branches."

He told them another parable. "The kingdom of heaven is like leaven which a woman took and hid in three measures of flour, till it was all leavened. . . .

"The kingdom of heaven is like treasure hidden in a field, which a man found and covered up; then in his joy he goes and sells all that he has and buys that field.

"Again, the kingdom of heaven is like a merchant in search of fine pearls, who, on finding one pearl of great value, went and sold all that he had and bought it.

"Again, the kingdom of heaven is like a net which was thrown into the sea and gathered fish of every kind; when it was full, men drew it ashore and sat down and sorted the good into vessels but threw away the bad. So it will be at the close of the age."

One of the most difficult things about believing in God is trying to talk about it. Someone asks you why you believe, or how

your life is different because you do, and there are no words
that are true enough, right enough, big enough to explain. You
rummage around for something to say, but everything sounds
either too vague or too pious. You could talk about how your
heart feels full to bursting sometimes, or about the mysterious
sense of kinship you feel with other human beings. You could
talk about how even the worst things that happen to you seem
to have a blessing hidden in them somewhere, but the truth is
that it is impossible to speak directly about holy things. How
can the language of earth capture the reality of heaven? How
can words describe that which is beyond all words? How can
human beings speak of God?

We do not do it well, that is for sure, but because we must
somehow try, we tend to talk about what we cannot say in terms
of what we can—that is, we tend to describe holy things by talking about ordinary things, and trusting each other to make the
connections. Believing in God is like coming home, we say, like
being born again. It is like jumping off the high dive, like getting struck by lightning, like falling in love. We cannot say what
it *is*, exactly, but we can say what it is *like*, and most of us get the
message.

If you still have your notes from high school English class,
you can probably find the section on figures of speech, where
this way of talking is called talking in *metaphors*—talking about
one thing by referring to another thing, getting at the meaning
of one thing by comparing it to another. Sometimes the comparisons are comfortable and familiar. Her eyes were as blue as
the sky, as blue as a robin's egg, as blue as the sea.

But other times the comparisons are jarring or startling. Her
eyes were as blue as a bruise, as blue as ink spilled on a white
page, as blue as a wave just before it breaks. When the comparisons catch us by surprise they make us stop, make us think.
How can these two things be alike? What do they have in common? How deep does this connection go? When the comparisons catch us by surprise, our everyday understanding of things
is broken open and we are invited to explore them all over
again, to go inside of them and see what is new.

Jesus did it all the time. Throughout the Gospels, and in

Matthew's Gospel in particular, he was always making comparisons. Sinners are like lost sheep, the word of God is like seed sown on different kinds of ground, the kingdom of heaven is like a wedding feast, God is like the owner of a vineyard. "The kingdom of heaven is like this. . . ." he said over and over again, telling his followers stories about brides and grooms, sheep and shepherds, wheat and tares.

Have you ever wondered why he taught that way? Why didn't he just come right out and say what he meant? If anyone in the world were qualified to speak directly about God, surely it was Jesus, and yet he too spoke indirectly, making surprising comparisons between holy things and ordinary things, breaking open our everyday understanding of things and inviting us to explore them all over again.

In the passage we have just heard, he launches a volley of such comparisons. The kingdom of heaven is like a mustard seed, he says, like yeast, like buried treasure, like a fine pearl, like a net cast into the sea. The images come quickly, one right after another, with no preparation, no explanation, no time for questions and answers. It is not like him to be in such a rush. He is usually a better storyteller than that, gathering his listeners around him and sliding into his tale with one of those time-honored introductions like "There once was a landowner . . ." or "There once was a king . . ." When he does, his followers settle down to listen, knowing that the story will be full of meaning for them, knowing that they had better listen well.

But these five flashes of the kingdom come at us so quickly that there is no time to settle down at all. Jesus zings us with them—one, two, three, four, five—like snapshots, like scenes glimpsed through the windows of a fast-moving train. The kingdom of heaven is like *this* and *this* and *this*, he says. It is almost like he does not want us to think too much about them, like he does not want us to get stuck on any one of them but to be dazzled by the number and variety of the things the kingdom of heaven is like—like *this* and *this* and *this*.

The first two comparisons seem easy enough. The kingdom of heaven is like a mustard seed or a handful of yeast—nothing much to look at, not very impressive at all, at least not at first.

But give either of them something to work on—sow the seed, mix the yeast with flour—and the results can be astounding: a tree big enough for birds to nest in, bread enough to feed the family for a month. If the kingdom of heaven is like that, then it is surprising, and potent, and more than meets the eye.

The next pair of comparisons is more difficult. First, the kingdom is like a man who finds buried treasure in a field, covers it back up, and sells all that he owns to buy the field. He is a poor man who becomes a rich man through luck. And second, the kingdom is like a merchant who searches for and finds a pearl of great price, selling all that *he* owns to buy *it*. He is a rich man who becomes a richer man through skill. But rich or poor, skillful or just plain lucky, each man finds something of great value and sells all that he has to make it his own. Each man finds something that makes everything else he owns trivial by comparison and he does not think twice about trading it all in. If the kingdom is like that, then it is rare but attainable, for those who are not only willing but eager to pay the price.

The final comparison—of the kingdom of heaven and a fishing net—takes a different tack altogether. Thrown into the sea, the net gathers fish of every kind, good and bad, which are sorted out once the net is full. If the kingdom of heaven is like that, then it is not, in the end, something we find but something that finds us and hauls us into the light.

It is a lot to digest at one sitting, but the striking thing about all of these images is their essential *hiddenness*—the mustard seed hidden in the ground, the yeast hidden in the dough, the treasure hidden in the field, the pearl hidden among all the other pearls, the net hidden in the depths of the sea. If the kingdom is like these, then it is not something readily apparent to the eye but something that must be searched for, something just below the surface of things waiting there to be discovered and claimed.

Information like that has always tantalized the human imagination. A retired school bus driver takes up rock collecting and spends his weekends at local flea markets looking for interesting stones. One day he picks up a round one, about the size of a walnut, and likes the way it feels in his hand. So he buys it and takes it home and polishes it up and shows it to his friend the jeweler, who tells him that what he has bought for a dollar and a half is a 250-carat ruby.

Or a poor single mother of three is notified of her maiden aunt's death in a distant city. Since she is the woman's only kin, she buys a bus ticket with the end of her grocery money and goes to sort through the old woman's things. Packing her aunt's old brown wool coat in a box for the Salvation Army, she feels something stiff down around the hem and discovers hundred-dollar bills sewn into the lining.

Or a young research librarian without an adventurous bone in his body is shelving old books one day when one falls apart in his hands. As he tries to stack all the loose pages back together again, a yellowed slip of paper falls out of the ruined binding. Picking it up off the floor and holding it to the light, he finds himself staring at an ancient map to Shangri-la, or the fountain of youth, or King Solomon's mines.

It is the stuff legends are made of—the sunken treasure, the secret knowledge, the long-lost masterpiece gathering dust in the attic—suddenly discovered, suddenly found and claimed and enjoyed amid much celebration. That is what the kingdom of heaven is like, Jesus says. Whether it begins as a seed hidden in the ground or a treasure hidden in a field, the kingdom comes when it is no longer hidden but revealed, when the tree is full grown, when the treasure chest is opened, when what was lost is found and what was secret is known and what was hidden away is brought forth for everyone to see.

It is exciting business, but where do we begin? Without a treasure map, or a maiden aunt, or much luck shopping for rubies, where do we start looking for the hidden kingdom of heaven? All of these metaphors are fine, all of these parables about seeds and yeast and nets are very interesting, but when it comes right down to hunting the honest-to-goodness kingdom of heaven, where are we supposed to start?

It seems like we ought to start some place really holy, some place really extraordinary, like a medieval monastery, maybe, translating ancient texts with biblical scholars; or in the slums of Calcutta, bathing the sick and the dying with Mother Teresa.

Maybe we should begin in the Holy Land, or at the Vatican, or the National Cathedral. Then again it may not matter *where* we are, exactly, as long as we keep our eyes open for extraordinary clues *wherever* we are—looking out for heavenly visions, listening out for heavenly voices. Because if the kingdom of heaven is hidden in this world, it is hidden really well, and only the most dedicated detectives among us stand a chance of finding it at all.

Unless, of course, God has resorted to the oldest trick in the book and hidden it in plain view. There is always that possibility, you know—that God decided to hide the kingdom of heaven not in any of the extraordinary places that treasure hunters would be sure to check but in the last place that any of us would think to look, namely, in the ordinary circumstances of our everyday lives: like a silver spoon in the drawer with the stainless, like a diamond necklace on the bureau with the rhinestones; the extraordinary hidden in the ordinary, the kingdom of heaven all mixed in with the humdrum and ho-hum of our days, as easy to find as an amaryllis bulb in the dark basement that suddenly sends forth a shoot, or a child's smile when she awakes from sleep, or the first thunderstorm after a long drought—all of them signs of the kingdom of heaven, clues to all the holiness hidden in the dullest of our days.

Jesus knew it all along. Why else would he talk about heaven in terms of farmers and fields and women baking bread and merchants buying and selling things and fishermen sorting fish, unless he meant somehow to be telling us that the kingdom of heaven has to do with these things, that our treasure is buried not in some exotic far-off place that requires a special map but that "X" marks the spot right here, right now, in all the ordinary people and places and activities of our lives?

If we want to speak of heavenly things, he seems to say, we may begin by speaking about earthly things, and if we want to describe that which is beyond all words, we may begin with words we know, words such as: *man, woman, field, seed, bird, air, yeast, bread*; words such as: *pearl, net, sea, fish, joy*. The kingdom is like these things; the kingdom is found in these things. These are the places to dig for the kingdom of heaven; these are the places to look for the will and rule and presence of God. If we cannot find them here we will never find them anywhere else, for earth is where the seeds of heaven are sown, and their treasure is the only one worth having.

7

The Problem with Miracles

Matthew 14:13–21

Now when Jesus heard this, he withdrew from there in a boat to a lonely place apart. But when the crowds heard it, they followed him on foot from the towns. As he went ashore he saw a great throng; and he had compassion on them, and healed their sick. When it was evening, the disciples came to him and said, "This is a lonely place, and the day is now over; send the crowds away to go into the villages and buy food for themselves." Jesus said, "They need not go away; you give them something to eat." They said to him, "We have only five loaves here and two fish." And he said, "Bring them here to me." Then he ordered the crowds to sit down on the grass; and taking the five loaves and the two fish he looked up to heaven, and blessed, and broke and gave the loaves to the disciples, and the disciples gave them to the crowds. And they all ate and were satisfied. And they took up twelve baskets full of the broken pieces left over. And those who ate were about five thousand men, besides women and children.

Each of the four Gospel writers records the life of Jesus in a different way. Picking and choosing from all the stories they knew about what their Lord said and did, each of them came up with a different combination. Only Matthew and Luke write about

Jesus' birth, for instance, while John is the only one who tells the story of Lazarus being raised from the dead. The Sermon on the Mount is found only in Matthew, and while Luke includes about half of the same sermon in his Gospel, he says that it took place on a wide plain.

But one thing that all four writers included in their Gospels is this morning's story about the miraculous feeding of the five thousand. It was too important a story to leave out—too important in the life of Jesus and too important in the life of the church. It was a story about Jesus' ability to provide for their needs, and not only for their spiritual needs but for their human needs as well. When they were sick, Jesus healed them; when they were sad, Jesus blessed them; when they were hungry, Jesus fed them.

In time, it became a story that early Christians told around the table when they gathered for worship. As they blessed, broke, and shared the miraculous bread of the Lord's Supper, they remembered that other time when bread was miraculously blessed, broken, and shared, and it was as if Jesus stood among them again, laying his hands on a little so that it became enough for all.

The feeding of the five thousand is a story that carries echoes of other stories, such as the Old Testament story about how manna fell from the sky to feed the children of Israel in the wilderness. That was the first bread miracle that God worked on their behalf. They were far away from home in that story too, without a clue where their next meal would come from, when God sent manna from heaven to fill their bellies and feed their trust in him. In the book of 2 Kings you can read the story of another bread miracle, in which the prophet Elisha fed a hundred hungry men with twenty barley loaves. His disciples protested that it was not enough to set before all those people, but Elisha insisted and the Lord provided, so that everyone ate his fill and there were leftovers besides.

So this morning's miracle story is one in a series of bread miracles in the Bible, and an impressive one at that. Jesus feeds five thousand men, Matthew tells us, not counting the women and children who are present. He feeds what amounts to a small town with five loaves and two fishes, a meal that multiplies until no one can eat any more and the scraps fill twelve baskets. It is a miracle, and perhaps that should be the end of that, but miracles tend to nag at those of us who do not experience them very often.

We tend to wonder things, like, how did it happen exactly? Did Jesus multiply the loaves all at once, so that the disciples had to recruit people to help them carry all that bread? Or did it happen as the loaves were being passed through the crowd? When someone tore off a chunk of bread, did the loaf suddenly grow? As you reached out to take the loaf, did it sort of jump in your hand and get bigger? Or did new loaves appear while no one was looking? Maybe you set yours down for a moment as you shifted your child from one arm to the other, and when you reached down to pick it up again, there were two loaves instead of one. How did it happen exactly?

Matthew does not tell us. What he does tell us is that the miracle happened at "a lonely place apart," which was where Jesus had gone after he heard the news that John the Baptist was dead, beheaded at the whim of a dancing girl. Having heard that, he wanted to be alone, and who could blame him? He had lost his prophet, the man who had baptized him and who had devoted his whole life to preparing the way of the Lord. And worse than that, he had lost him to murder, a vivid reminder to Jesus and everyone else that God's prophets were not immune to death, that if anything they were more likely to die violently than quietly, and sooner than later.

It was very bad news, and when Jesus heard it he withdrew in a boat to a lonely place apart, but when the crowds heard it they followed him on foot from the towns. He may have needed to be alone, but they had needs of their own. They were sick, they were sad, they were hungry, and while anyone but the son of God might have ordered them to get lost, Jesus had compassion on them. His heart went out to them, and he spent the afternoon walking among them, laying his hands on them and saying the things they needed to hear.

When evening fell, the disciples found him and suggested that he send everyone away to buy supper in one of the nearby

villages. They meant no harm; they were simply being practical. Night was falling, they were out in the middle of nowhere,
and their stomachs were beginning to growl. It was time to call
it a day, time to build a campfire and eat the little bit of food
they had brought with them. It was time to take care of themselves for a change, and to suggest that everyone else do the
same thing.

But Jesus had a better idea. "They need not go away," he
said, seeming to know that what the crowd needed more than a
hot meal was to stay together, seeming to know that there was
more nourishment for them in each other's company than in
some neighboring farmer's goat cheese or boiled rice. Sometimes, after very bad news, it does not matter *what* you eat as
long as you eat it *with* someone.

"They need not go away," Jesus said to his disciples. "You
give them something to eat." I wish I had been there. I wish I
could have seen how they looked at each other when he said
that. Give them something to eat? Us? You are in charge here,
Jesus; you are the boss. What do you mean, *we* should give
them something to eat? All we have between us is five loaves
and two salted fish, which is hardly a snack for twelve men,
never mind five thousand. There are *five thousand people* out
there, Jesus. No disrespect intended, but you are not making
sense.

He may not have been making sense, but then again he may
have had a sense of the situation that went beyond the disciples'
common sense. They were, after all, operating out of a sense of
scarcity. They looked at the crowd, saw no picnic baskets or
backpacks, and assumed that no one had anything to eat. They
looked at their own meager resources and assumed that it was
not enough to go around their own circle, much less to feed the
whole crowd.

But Jesus operated out of a different set of assumptions. If
the disciples operated out of a sense of scarcity, then what Jesus
operated out of was a sense of plenty. He looked at the same
things the disciples looked at, but where they saw not enough,
he saw plenty: plenty of time, plenty of food, and plenty of pos-
sibilities with the resources at hand. Not that he knew how it

was all going to work out exactly—he was human, remember, as well as divine—but what Jesus knew beyond a shadow of a doubt was that wherever there was plenty of God there would be plenty of everything else.

So he asked the disciples to bring their food to him, and he ordered the crowd to sit down on the grass, and he proceeded to bless five loaves and two fishes in front of them all, perfectly confident that God would turn not enough into plenty. Can you imagine what it must have been like to watch him do that? To be sitting in that crowd, watching a rabbi bless five loaves, and break them, and give them to his disciples to give to a crowd that went on forever? They did not know they were in for a miracle, after all, and anyone could do the arithmetic: five loaves divided by five thousand equals one loaf per thousand people.

Unless you were on the front row, chances are you might not have seen him at all. You might have had to punch your neighbor and say, "What's going on up there?" and he might have said, "You're not going believe it—that Jesus fellow just said grace over five loaves and two fish and now some of his men are passing them out through the crowd. It's the craziest thing I've ever seen, but don't get excited—it will all be gone before it ever gets to us."

Some of the crowd must have laughed out loud, while some of them were mystified and still others were embarrassed for Jesus, that he should have promised so much with so little to deliver. But I wonder if some of them were not touched, too—touched by the way the disciples handed over all they had, and touched by Jesus' simple confidence that it would be enough. I wonder if they did not look at that small basket of food going around and feel the food hidden in their own pockets begin to burn holes in them. Because you know they had some—a bit of lamb wrapped in a grape leaf, a few raisins, a chunk of bread left over from breakfast. You know some of them had tucked a little something away before heading off on foot to a lonely place apart. Wouldn't you have done the same thing? But it would not have been enough to share, so chances are that those with something to eat kept it hidden—wrapped in a handkerchief, stuffed up a sleeve—waiting for an opportune moment to go off for a walk alone and sneak a bite.

And it might have worked, too. They might have been able to keep their own food for themselves if that bread basket had not come around, full of scraps, everyone so careful not to break off too much, everyone wanting Jesus' crazy idea to work so much that very carefully, very secretly, they all began to put their own bread in the basket, reaching in as if they were taking some out and leaving some behind instead, so that the meal grew and grew, so that when the disciples collected the broken pieces at the end they stared in amazement at twelve baskets full of bread—wheat bread, sourdough, pumpernickel, rye, raisin bread, pita bread, bagels, and maybe even an oat bran muffin or two—every kind of bread you can think of, the leftovers from a meal for five thousand that started off with five blessed and broken loaves.

But that is not a miracle! Isn't that what you are thinking? That is just human beings being generous, sharing what they have—even when it is not much, even when it is not enough to go around. That is not a miracle! That is just a whole crowd of people moving from a sense of scarcity to a sense of plenty—overcoming their fear of going hungry, giving up their need to protect themselves. That is just people refusing to play the age-old game of what-is-mine-is-mine-and-what-is-yours-is-yours, people turning their pockets inside out for one another without worrying about what is in it for them. That is not a miracle! Or is it?

The problem with miracles is that we tend to get mesmerized by them, focusing on God's responsibility and forgetting our own. Miracles let us off the hook. They appeal to the part of us that is all too happy to let God feed the crowd, save the world, do it all. We do not have what it takes, after all. What we have to offer is not enough to make any difference at all, so we hold back and wait for a miracle, looking after our own needs and looking for God to help those who cannot help themselves.

Sitting in the crowd, waiting for God to act, we can hang on to our own little loaves of bread. They are not much; they would not go far. Besides, if Jesus is in charge of the bread, doesn't that excuse us from sharing our own? God will provide; let God provide. "Send the crowds away to go into the villages," the disciples say, "and buy food for themselves."

"They need not go away," Jesus says. "You give them something to eat." Not me but you; not my bread but yours; not sometime or somewhere else but right here and now. Stop looking for someone else to solve the problem and solve it yourselves. Stop waiting for food to fall from the sky and share what you have. Stop waiting for a miracle and participate in one instead.

Bring what you have to me; that is where to begin. Remember that there is no such thing as "your" bread or "my" bread; there is only "our" bread, as in "give us this day our daily bread." However much you have, just bring it to me and believe that it is enough to begin with, enough to get the ball rolling, enough to start a trend. Be the first in the crowd to turn your pockets inside out; be the first on your block to start a miracle.

No one knows how it really happened. Your guess is as good as mine, but what Jesus has been saying to his followers forever he goes on saying to us today: "They need not go away; you give them something to eat." If it is a saying that strikes fear in our hearts, that makes the loaves we have seem like nothing at all, we have only to remember what he says next: "Bring them here to me."

8

Saved by Doubt

Matthew 14:22–33

Jesus made the disciples get into the boat and go before him to the other side, while he dismissed the crowds. And after he had dismissed the crowds, he went up into the hills by himself to pray. When evening came, he was there alone, but the boat by this time was many furlongs distant from the land, beaten by the waves; for the wind was against them. And in the fourth watch of the night he came to them, walking on the sea. But when the disciples saw him walking on the sea, they were terrified, saying, "It is a ghost!" And they cried out for fear. But immediately he spoke to them, saying, "Take heart, it is I; have no fear."

And Peter answered him, "Lord, if it is you, bid me come to you on the water." He said, "Come." So Peter got out of the boat and walked on the water and came to Jesus; but when he saw the wind, he was afraid, and beginning to sink he cried out, "Lord, save me." Jesus immediately reached out his hand and caught him, saying to him, "O man of little faith, why did you doubt?" And when they got into the boat, the wind ceased. And those in the boat worshiped him, saying, "Truly you are the Son of God."

Today's story about Peter's brief walk on the water appears only in the Gospel according to Matthew. Mark includes the story about Jesus coming across the sea and calming the storm, John uses an even shorter version of it, and Luke leaves it out altogether. The three Gospel writers who tell the story agree that it followed the feeding of the five thousand and that Jesus' calming of the storm was a miracle worked for the disciples alone—a very unusual occurrence in the New Testament.

They also share an ancient understanding of the sea as the abode of demonic forces, as the place on earth where chaos still reigns, which makes Jesus' walk across it all that much more miraculous. By strolling across the stormy sea of Galilee as if it were a paved street, he really does beat down Satan under his feet, proving his dominion over the devils of the deep as well as the wild winds and crashing waves up above. The Lord of humankind is also the Lord of wind, sea, earth, and fire, whom the elements obey without a word having been spoken.

But only Matthew mentions Peter, which may be why his version of the story is the most popular one. There is something so appealing about Peter: the brash, passionate disciple who is always rushing into things, saying what the others are only thinking, and doing what the others would not dare. Peter is Jesus' first disciple, and clearly one of his favorites. When Jesus hikes to the Mount of the Transfiguration later on in Matthew, Peter is one of the three disciples whom he asks to go with him, and while the other two are dumbfounded by the sight of Jesus talking with Moses and Elijah, it is Peter who blurts out, "Lord, if you wish, I will make three booths here, one for you and one for Moses and one for Elijah" (Matt. 17:4). What a stupid thing to say! But what a human thing to say.

It is Peter who asks Jesus to explain his parables, Peter who answers Jesus' questions first, Peter who understands Jesus' true identity but fails to understand what it will cost him, and Peter whom Jesus calls the foundation rock of the church, one moment before he also calls him Satan, who is not on the side of God but of men (Matt. 16:23).

It is Peter who swears he will never deny Jesus, and Peter who does; it is Peter whom Jesus asks to pray with him in the garden of Gethsemane, and Peter who falls asleep. And in today's story, it is Peter whom Jesus calls to walk with him upon the water, and Peter who sinks. Over and over and over again, he is the disciple who takes risks, who makes great leaps of faith and stumbles as often as not but who keeps brushing himself off and getting up to try, try again.

It is hard not to love Peter. Sure, he is one of those enthusiastic types who talk a better game than they play, but still there is something so sincere about him, and so achingly familiar. He is full of faith one minute and full of doubt the next, riding high on his confidence in Jesus one moment and lying in the dirt the next. He is not a fake. Through all his ups and downs, all his great moments and his awful ones, Peter's heart is on his sleeve. What you see is what you get with him: an impetuous, outspoken man who both loves Jesus and lets him down, who richly deserves Jesus' judgment but who also receives his grace.

No wonder Matthew likes him. At the beginning of today's story, Peter is just one of the crowd. Weary after the feeding of the five thousand, Jesus has sent his disciples on ahead of him and has gone by himself into the mountains to pray. By nightfall, he is still at it, while out on the sea his disciples have their hands full, trying to steer their little boat right into a high wind and higher waves.

They are all, presumably, soaked, their teeth chattering and their hands blistered from their efforts, when Jesus comes to them. It is around three in the morning, Matthew says. No one can sleep, even if he wants to. They are all watching the horizon, looking for land, measuring the distance they have come against the distance they still have to go when someone spots a shadowy figure walking toward them across the boiling water.

"It's a ghost!" someone cries, but immediately the ghost speaks to them, saying, "Take heart, it is I; have no fear." His voice must sound strange to them, or perhaps he is still too far away to see, because Peter does not trust him. Scared to death, putting into words what the others hardly dare think, Peter says, "Lord, if it is you, bid me come to you on the water."

Now that is a strange thing to say. Why not say, "Lord, if it is you, tell us what we all had for supper tonight," or "Lord, if it is you, make this storm stop right now"? But neither of those is the test that Peter proposes. "Lord," he says, "if it is you, bid me come to you on the water." Bid me come to where you are; let me join you on the water. Show me that what you can do, I can do, if only you tell me to. Take away my doubt. Make me have faith.

"Come," Jesus says, so Peter swings his legs over the side of the boat and, while all the other disciples watch with their hearts beating in their mouths, he places his feet on the surface of the water—the waves crashing against the side of the boat, the wind whipping his hair into his eyes—he puts his feet flat on top of the water, takes a huge, trembling breath, and stands. Then he takes a few hesitant steps toward Jesus across the heaving surface, like the first steps he ever took in his life, and he is doing fine until a gust of wind almost topples him, and he gets scared, and feels his feet sinking into the black waves below, and he goes down like a stone.

Even if you have never tried to walk on water, you know how he felt. Maybe you were crossing a stream on a fallen log, inching your way across its rough, rounded surface, doing just fine until you looked down at the rushing water below you and got frightened, and lost your balance, and had to drag yourself the rest of the way by the seat of your pants.

Or maybe you were learning to ride a bicycle, and had gained enough speed so that suddenly you stopped wobbling and started flying, the wind in your hair, the scenery whipping by, when just as suddenly you lost your confidence, dropped one foot on the ground, and brought the whole experiment crashing down on top of you.

Or maybe you were addressing a crowd, standing up in front of them to say something you believed in, and at first the words just flowed from your mouth, exactly the words you needed at exactly the moment you needed them, and then you looked at all those faces looking back at you, and you lost your nerve, and your brain turned to mush, and you sat down as quickly as you could, your cheeks burning, your hands sweating, and your heart making noise in your ears.

"Lord, save me," Peter cries out, and Jesus does, reaching out his hand and catching him, hauling him out of the cold water like a big, frightened fish and dragging him over to where the other disciples can pull him back into the boat. And then the awful words: "O man of little faith," Jesus says to Peter, "why did you doubt?"

They are the words none of us ever wants to hear addressed to us, and yet they are the same words many of us ask ourselves every day. Why don't I have more faith? Why can't I trust God? Why am I afraid to let go and let God care for me? Why do I doubt? I believe I am in God's hands and that they are good hands, but then I lose my job and cannot find another, and as the interviews go on and on and my savings disappear, my faith goes with them and I begin to sink.

I believe that God is present and active in the world, but terrible things keep happening. I read the newspaper headlines, the crime statistics, the obituaries, and it seems like the storm will never end. I believe in life after death and a bright future with God, but then I get sick and the doctor says six, maybe nine months, and I pray for a miracle but no miracle comes, and I pray for the reassuring voice of God but no voice comes, and the waves creep up my legs, and I begin to sink.

Why do we doubt? Because we are afraid, because the sea is so vast and we are so small, because the storm is so powerful and we are so easily sunk, because life is so beyond our control and we are so helpless in its grip. Why do we doubt? Because we are afraid, even when we *do* have faith. Because we do have faith, you know. We do not have none; we have some. Like Peter, we have a little, and a little is better than nothing, even though there are times when it does not seem enough to save us.

Like Peter, we have faith and we doubt, we try to walk with Jesus and we fail, we take a few steps and we sink, we cry out "Lord, save me!" and he does, giving us both his hand and his rebuke: "O you of little faith, why did you doubt?" Hearing that, most of us count ourselves failures, but I wonder. Can you imagine the story turning out any other way?

What if Peter had not sunk? What if he had jumped out of the boat with perfect confidence, landed splat with both feet flat on the water and smiled across the waves at Jesus, gliding toward him without a moment's hesitation? What if the other disciples had followed suit, piling out of the boat after him, and all of them, with perfect faith, had romped on the water while the storm raged and the wind beat the sails and lightning split the dark night above their heads?

It would be a different story. It might even be a better story, but it would not be a story about us. The truth about us is more complicated. The truth about us is that we obey and fear, we walk and sink, we believe and doubt. But it is not like we do only one or the other. We do both. Our faith and our doubt are not mutually exclusive; they both exist in us at the same time, buoying us up and bearing us down, giving us courage and feeding our fears, supporting our weight on the wild seas of our lives and sinking us like stones.

This is why we need Jesus. This is why we would not be caught dead on the water without him. Our fears and doubts may paralyze us, but they are also what make us cry out for his saving touch, so how can they be all bad? If we never sank—if we could walk on the water just fine all by ourselves—we would not need a savior. We could go into business for ourselves. Our doubts, fearsome as they are, remind us who we are, and whose we are, and whom we need in our lives to save our lives. When we sink, as Peter does, as we all do, our Lord reaches out and catches us, responding first with grace, and then with judgment—"Why did you doubt?"—but *never* with rejection. He returns us to the boat, knowing full well that the only reason we are in the boat in the first place is because we believe, or want to believe, and because we mean to follow him through all our doubtful days.

He returns us to the boat, where our companions grab us by the scruff of the neck and haul us aboard, where we fall grateful and exhausted onto the slippery deck. All at once the wind ceases, and the waves hush, and in the awesome silence of that night becoming day, all of us who are in this boat together worship him, saying, "Truly, you are the Son of God."

9

Crossing the Line

Matthew 15:21–28

Jesus went away from there and withdrew to the district of Tyre and Sidon. And behold, a Canaanite woman from that region came out and cried, "Have mercy on me, O Lord, Son of David; my daughter is severely possessed by a demon." But he did not answer her a word. And his disciples came and begged him, saying, "Send her away, for she is crying after us." He answered, "I was sent only to the lost sheep of the house of Israel." But she came and knelt before him, saying, "Lord, help me." And he answered, "It is not fair to take the children's bread and throw it to the dogs." She said, "Yes, Lord, yet even the dogs eat the crumbs that fall from their master's table." Then Jesus answered her, "O woman, great is your faith! Be it done for you as you desire." And her daughter was healed instantly.

This passage from Matthew describes one of those difficult moments in Jesus' life that we might skip altogether if the lectionary did not direct us to deal with it. What makes it so difficult is how harsh Jesus sounds, how harsh and downright rude. First he refuses to answer a woman pleading for his help, then he denies that he has anything to offer "her kind," and finally he likens her to a dog before the sheer force of her faith changes something in him and he decides to answer her prayer after all.

The problem is that she is a Canaanite, one of the great unwashed with whom observant Jews of Jesus' time had little contact. She comes from the coastal region of Syria, where strange gods are worshiped and ritual laws of cleanliness are unknown. She is a Gentile, in other words, which is the biblical term for everyone who is not a Jew, and as such she is both an outsider and an untouchable.

Earlier, in the tenth chapter of Matthew, it is Jesus himself who warns his disciples to steer clear of Gentiles, reminding them that they have been sent only to the lost sheep of Israel. The only catch is that the lost sheep do not seem to want to be found. In spite of Jesus' undivided attention to them, they are not rushing to respond to his shepherd's call.

In today's story he has just come from Nazareth, his own hometown, where his friends and family have doubted his authority and taken offense at his teaching. He has recently received word that John the Baptist has lost his head to a dancing girl, and he has tried at this blow to withdraw from the crowds for a while, but the crowds have followed him, and he has, with five loaves and two fishes, fed them all. Then there was the storm at sea and Peter's wish to cross the water, ruined by Peter's fear and doubt. Everywhere Jesus turns he finds need—need and people who want what he can do for them but who remain blind to who he is. He is at the frayed end of his rope, and all but used up.

Then comes this Canaanite woman crying out to him to heal her daughter—one more of the needy multitudes who want something from him—only this one does a shocking thing: She calls him by name, "O Lord, Son of David." It is the title reserved for the Messiah, the title his own people have withheld from him. When this woman addresses him as the Son of David, she names something in him that even his own disciples have failed to recognize, and it must seem like a mean trick of fate to him to hear what he most wants to hear coming from the mouth of someone he least wants to hear it from.

So he does not answer her a word. He draws the line, as

surely as if he had leaned down and traced it in the dust at his feet. Enough is enough. He will go no further. The bank is closed. The doctor is out. The sign on the door says, "Closed for Business." So what if she called him by name? He will not waste his energy on this Gentile woman while his own people go wanting. "I was sent only to the lost sheep of the house of Israel," he says to the woman, and that is supposed to be that.

But the woman will not stay on her side of the line. Kneeling at his feet, she says, "Lord, help me." Jesus has dismissed her, but she will not be dismissed; she has gotten her foot in the door before Jesus can close it in her face, and she shows no sign of leaving before he has dealt with her. "Lord, help me," she says, and I can only imagine that his blood pressure goes up. Can't she hear? He has told her no, told her that she is not his sheep, but she does not seem to have gotten the message so he says it again, louder and clearer than before. "It is not fair to take the children's bread and throw it to the dogs," he says, a cruel rebuff if there ever was one.

Since Jesus was a human being as well as the son of God, it seems fair to guess what might have been going on with him. He was discouraged and weary and a long way from home. Every time he turned around someone wanted something from him, but at the same time no one wanted what he most wanted to give—namely, himself, in terms of *who* he was for them and not only in terms of what he could *do* for them.

It is not hard to imagine how that feels, even if you do not happen to be the Messiah—to be surrounded by appetites, by people who want your money and your time and your gifts but who do not seem much interested in who you really are; to be confused about what you are supposed to do, how much you are supposed to give, and to be worried about whether there is enough of you to go around.

The telephone rings and it is the Disabled American Veterans selling light bulbs, or the fire department recruiting sponsors for handicapped children, or the kidney foundation seeking donations. The doorbell rings and it is a sad-eyed man in overalls looking for work, while his whole family waits and watches from the battered car by the curb. Every day's mail brings more pleas for help from every cause under the sun: animal rights, the environment, child abuse prevention, Native Americans, civil liberties, cancer prevention.

You have to draw a line somewhere. You have to decide what you can do and what you cannot do, whom you can help and whom you cannot help, or you will be eaten alive. You will be swallowed whole and you may never even be missed, because everything you have is not enough to feed the hunger of the world. That is a point most of us reach, anyhow, and often we decide to draw the line around our own families and friends, around our own churches and communities and concerns.

We draw the line and, like Jesus, we may lose our tempers when outsiders try to cross it, because they are challenging the limits we have placed on ourselves to protect ourselves. Strangers show up saying, "Help me," and we invoke the line, the line that separates insiders from outsiders, clean from unclean, family from the wolves that howl outside our doors. "It is not fair to take the children's bread and throw it to the dogs," we say, or something to that effect. It sounds harsh, but what are you going to do? You have to draw the line somewhere.

But the Canaanite woman simply will not budge. Her responses to Jesus remind me of that game children play, in which two of them look steadily into each other's eyes, each trying to make the other blink first. Jesus all but claps his hands in the woman's face, but she does not blink. "Yes, Lord," she says when he calls her a dog, "yet even the dogs eat the crumbs that fall from their master's table." When she says that, something in Jesus snaps. He blinks. His anger dissolves. Something in him is rearranged and changed forever, a change you can hear in his voice. "O woman, great is your faith," he says to her. "Be it done for you as you desire." And her daughter is healed instantly.

The line he had drawn between him and the woman disappears; the limits he had placed on himself vanish, and you can almost hear the huge wheel of history turning as Jesus comes to a new understanding of who he is and what he has been called to do. He is no longer a Messiah called only to the lost sheep of

Israel, but God's chosen redeemer of the whole world, Jews and Gentiles alike, beginning with this Canaanite woman.

Through *her* faith he learns that God's purpose for him is bigger than he had imagined, that there *is* enough of him to go around, and in that moment there is no going back to the limits he observed even a moment ago. The old boundaries will not contain his new vision; he must rub them out and draw them bigger, to include this foreign woman today and who knows what tomorrow. It looks like answering God's call means that he can no longer control his ministry or narrow his mission. There is no more safety or certainty for him, no more guarding against loss or hanging on to his cherished notions about the way things ought to be. Faith works like a lever on him, opening his arms wider and wider until there is room for the whole world in them, until he allows them to be *nailed* open on the cross.

Isn't that the way it goes? Over and over, God's call to us means pushing old boundaries, embracing outsiders, giving up the notion that there is not enough of us to go around. We may resist; we may even lose our tempers, but the call of God is insistent, as insistent as the Canaanite woman who would not leave Jesus alone. The call of God keeps after us, calling us by name, until finally we step over the lines we have drawn for ourselves and discover a whole new world on the other side.

For me, one of God's most insistent calls has been to care for people with AIDS. At first I was afraid of them: afraid to visit them, afraid to touch them, afraid to hold their hands. I would stand outside a hospital room and read all the rules posted on the door about wearing gloves and masks and washing my hands with Betadine both when I went into the room and again when I left. That was in the old days, when we were all more afraid of AIDS because we knew less about how it was spread.

These days my fear is not about catching the disease. The sign on the door is gone, and I know that you cannot get AIDS from a hospital call. These days my fear is not about touching but about being touched—emotionally, that is, not physically. These days I hesitate outside a hospital room because I know that when I go inside I will come face to face with a frightened human being who is sick unto death and who needs all the care he or she can get. I know that I am going to face my own fear of death, and especially of dying young and alone. I know that I am going to face questions about God's role in such an illness. I know that my relationship with that person is going to require a lot of me, and I worry that there will not be enough of me— that I will not visit often enough, or offer enough hope, or find enough of the right words to say.

So whenever I hear about someone new with AIDS, some- one who has just found out or has just fallen ill and who is look- ing for someone to talk to, I want to draw the line. I want to say I am busy. I want to refer that person to someone else. I want to say that I only care for people in my own congregation. I get angry at the person for having AIDS, and at myself for being such a coward, and at God for allowing any of it to happen in the first place. I try to draw the line, but of course it does not work. God's insistent call keeps after me until I am knocking on a new door, and it opens, and I step across the threshold into a relationship about which I know nothing except that it will change my life. And that has been true, because in every case I have gotten more than I have given. I have gotten to know peo- ple whose pain and fear have opened them up to God like never before, and who have taught me what it means to live on the daily bread of faith, without a clue what will happen tomorrow. I have watched people sort through their lives, giving thanks for the wheat and burning the chaff and knowing the difference between the two. I have watched people die with as much courage as they lived—these untouchables, these outsiders— whom I would never have known if I had stayed on my side of the line and insisted that they stay on theirs.

The best lesson, I suppose, is that God's face can turn up anywhere, and especially on the far side of the lines we draw to protect ourselves: in the face of a Canaanite woman, or a per- son with AIDS, or in any of the other faces that turn toward us seeking help, seeking care, seeking relationship with us that we are reluctant to give. The call of God is insistent, and whenever we limit who we will be to other people or who we will let them be for us, God gets to work, rubbing out the lines we have drawn around ourselves and calling us into the limitless country of his love. We may well formulate new limits and draw new lines, but none of them last very long, because that is the way it is when people have been called out by God. Once God has called us out there is no going back—whatever we choose to do. God never calls us back behind our lines.

What does that mean, day to day? It means noticing the difference between the times we are hanging back, clinging to our limits, and the times we are moving out, pushing into new and often frightening territory. It is a difference you can *feel*: the difference between withdrawing from people, failing to meet their eyes, keeping a tight rein on your feelings, protecting yourself. It is the difference between that and putting yourself in the paths of strangers, being the first to extend your hand, aching with empathy for a world in travail, trying new things, changing your mind.

It can be a painful difference, to be sure—as painful as it was for Jesus to hear a Canaanite call him Lord when his own family would not; as painful as it was for him to step beyond generations of tradition and respond to her faith; as painful as it is for any one of us to step over the lines we have drawn to protect ourselves and explore unknown terrain.

Let go! Step out! Look a Canaanite in the eye, knock on a strange door, ask an outsider what his life is like, trespass an old boundary, enter a new relationship, push a limit, take a risk, give up playing it safe! You have nothing to lose but your life the way it has been, and there is lots more life where that came from. And if you get scared, which you will, and if you get mad, which you probably will too, remember today's story. With Jesus as our model—and our Lord—we are called to step over the lines we have drawn for ourselves, not because we have to, and not because we ought to, or even because we want to, but because we know that it is God's own self who waits for us on the other side.

10

God's Rock

Matthew 16:13–20

Now when Jesus came into the district of Caesarea Philippi, he asked his disciples, "Who do men say that the Son of man is?" And they said, "Some say John the Baptist, others say Elijah, and others Jeremiah or one of the prophets." He said to them, "But who do you say that I am?" Simon Peter replied, "You are the Christ, the Son of the living God." And Jesus answered him, "Blessed are you, Simon Bar-Jona! For flesh and blood has not revealed this to you, but my Father who is in heaven. And I tell you, you are Peter, and on this rock I will build my church, and the powers of death shall not prevail against it. I will give you the keys of the kingdom of heaven, and whatever you bind on earth shall be bound in heaven, and whatever you loose on earth shall be loosed in heaven." Then he strictly charged the disciples to tell no one that he was the Christ.

Several years ago, a woman I know walked out of her church after a particularly rousing Sunday service and bumped into a thin, sort of lost-looking man who was standing on the sidewalk looking up at the cross on top of the church steeple. She excused herself and started to walk away, but the man called her back. "Tell me," he said, pointing through the front doors into the church she had belonged to most of her life, "what is it that you believe in there?" She started to answer him and then realized that she did not *know* the answer, or did not know how to put it into words, and as she stood there trying to compose something the man said, "Never mind. I'm sorry if I bothered you," and walked away.

He *did* bother her, and her story bothered me as I tried to decide what I would have answered in her place. Why *do* I go to church, and what *is* it that we believe in there? The Nicene Creed? That is not exactly the sort of answer you want to recite on a sidewalk, even if you think someone might stick around until you are finished. That Jesus is my Lord? Sure, but what does that mean to a man on the sidewalk? That in spite of all appearances to the contrary, the world is in God's good hands? Says who? So what? What is it that we believe?

In this morning's lesson Jesus himself is the man on the sidewalk, the one who asks the question about what it all means, about what *he* means. He and his disciples have just come into the district of Caesarea Philippi trailing miracles behind them: the feeding of the four and five thousand, the calming of the storm at sea, the curing of the Canaanite woman's daughter, among many others. But Jesus has not just been healing; he has been teaching as well, lessons about obedience to the law and about the difference between words and deeds and about reading the signs of the times.

Every now and then he quizzes his disciples to see how much they are taking in, to see how well they have understood him, and he does not hide his displeasure at their consistently low scores. In the verses just before the ones we are addressing today, he warns them to be on guard against the yeast of the Pharisees and Sadducees. Eager to please, they put their literal, fishermen's heads together and decide that Jesus is talking about bread. "We brought no bread," one of them says, and Jesus explodes. "O men of little faith," he says, "why do you discuss among yourselves the fact that you have no bread? . . . How is it that you fail to perceive that I did not speak about bread?" (Matt. 16:8–11).

Small wonder, then, that they are a little anxious when Jesus gathers them all around and asks an entirely different kind of question—not one about anything he has said, but one about who he is. "Who do men say the Son of man is?" he asks them, and they are relieved, because it is a question they have some answers to. "John the Baptist," one of them answers, while the others rummage around in their heads for what they have heard. "Elijah," someone else suggests. "Jeremiah," says another, "or one of the prophets." They pull the names out of their pockets like interesting stones they have found and hand them over to Jesus for appraisal. There is no great risk involved in repeating what you have *heard*, after all, in reporting what others have said *they* believe. This is just a consultation among friends, a staff meeting for the purpose of deciding how Jesus' ministry is going. Some people believe he is John the Baptist resurrected, some that he is Elijah or one of the other prophets due to appear near the end of the world.

You can almost see the expectation on the disciples' faces as they turn over the tidbits they have heard. So which is it, Lord? What is the right answer? A, B, C, or none of the above? But Jesus does not give them his answer; what he wants are *their* answers, and again, you can almost see their faces when he turns the question back on them. "But who do you say that I am?" he asks them, they who are his nearest and dearest, they who have received the best he has to offer, who are his own. Who do *you* say I am? What is it that you believe in there?

It is too bad that the Bible has not come down to us like a musical score with all the pauses written in, or like the script of a play that tells us what happens while nothing is being said. It would be helpful to have stage directions, something like: [*Center stage: As soon as Jesus asks the question the disciples all look away, some of them studying the backs of their hands while others move little piles of dirt around with the toes of their sandals.*] Who knows how long that silence lasts before Peter breaks it with his answer? "You are the Christ, the son of the living God."

Thank goodness for Peter! Right or wrong, he is always the first one out of the gate, the first one to leave his fish net and follow Jesus, the first one out of the boat to walk on the water, the first to volunteer his opinion on any given subject. Sometimes it is hard to say whether he is courageous or just plain reckless, but in any case his answer is apparently the one Jesus is looking for, because in one fell swoop Jesus pronounces Peter blessed, the rock upon which the church will be built, and the inheritor of the keys to the kingdom of heaven.

It sort of makes you want to have your own answer ready just in case you are given a similar opportunity to win the sweepstakes, but there is a catch, because while Peter's answer seems to be the right one, it is not really his. "Blessed are you," Jesus tells him, "for flesh and blood has not revealed this to you, but my Father who is in heaven," which is a little like saying, "Blessed are you for an answer that is not your own." If it was not even Peter's answer, if he did not even think it up, then why does he get rewarded for it?

His sudden promotion may have seemed a bit odd to the other disciples as well. Peter *sank* in the middle of his walk across the water, after all, and while he may have been the first with his hand in the air when a question was asked, he did not always follow through on his bold pronouncements.

"You are Peter," Jesus says, giving Simon Bar-Jona a new name, "and on this rock I will build my church," but six sentences later Jesus will stub his toe on that same rock, for no sooner does Peter receive his new authority than he begins to argue with Jesus about what is going to happen in Jerusalem. "Get behind me, Satan," Jesus finally says to him in next week's reading. "You are a stumbling block in my path." Peter goes from being blessed to being satanic, from being the cornerstone of the church to being a stumbling block in Christ's way. What does it all mean? How can Peter be the rock with the right answer and the devil in the way all at the same time? And if he is, then what in the world is it that we are supposed to learn from him?

It is almost impossible to squeeze a moral lesson out of this story, to find some model for our own behavior, because the fact is that Peter does not on his own do anything particularly right. He is impulsive and opinionated, and when push comes to shove he denies that he knows Jesus at all. About all that can be said in his favor is that he is willing to go first, to speak his mind, and that every time he falls down he gets back up again, brushes himself off, and charges ahead. While the other disciples hang back for fear of giving the wrong answer, Peter risks his own answer, which, lo and behold, turns out to be God's answer, and sweet music to Jesus' ears.

"You are *Petros*," Jesus says to him, making a pun in his native tongue, "and on this *petra* I will build my church." It is the same word he uses twice, the masculine and then the feminine form of the word for "rock," but there is a subtle difference between the two. *Petros*—the name Jesus gives Peter—means a stone or a pebble, a small piece of a larger rock, while *petra* means a boulder, a mother lode, a great big rock. So that makes Peter a chip off the old block, a piece of the rock, against which the powers of death shall not prevail.

It is nothing that he is or says or does all by himself that wins him the keys to the kingdom. He is blessed because his answer is God's answer, and he is a rock because he is a chunk off the Rock of Ages, and it is on this *relationship* that the church is built, not on any virtue of Peter's—or yours, or mine. Peter is chosen, but not because the right answer has occurred to him. On the contrary, the right answer has occurred to him because he is chosen, because Jesus in his unsearchable wisdom, his inscrutable way, decided to pick a bullheaded, bighearted, fallible, stubborn, never-say-die rock upon which to build his church.

Peter may not exhibit the flawless character, the intellectual profundity, the spiritual depth I would prefer in the founder of my church, but I will tell you this: I am really glad to hear that he is the one in charge of heaven's gates. Someone like him may understand someone like me—someone who finds answers hard to come by, who finds it easier and safer to repeat other people's answers—because I have not thought about my own, or because my own do not sound good enough, or because I do not trust God to help me with them. Peter may understand someone who goes ahead and says things and then regrets them, or makes brave promises, like, "Even if I must die with you, I will not deny you" (Matt. 26:35) and then loses heart, saying not once but three times, "I do not know the man" (Matt. 26:74).

If Peter is the rock upon which the church is built, then there is hope for all of us, because he is one of us, because he remains God's chosen rock whether he is acting like a cornerstone or a stumbling block, and because he shows us that blessedness is less about perfectness than about willingness—that what counts is to risk our own answers, to go ahead and try, to get up one more time than we fall.

The story of Peter's last encounter with Jesus is told not by Matthew but by John. It takes place on a beach, where the risen Lord has just cooked breakfast for his disciples. As soon as the meal is over, Jesus turns to Peter and asks him, not once but three times, "Do you love me?" Three times Peter answers, "Yes, Lord; you know that I love you." And three times Jesus replies, "Feed my sheep" (John 21:15–17), which leads you to think that maybe the final answer Jesus seeks from those who love him is not an answer that is spoken so much as one that is lived, that the real truth about who he is for each one of us shows up not on our lips but in our lives.

So the next time you bump into someone who asks you what you believe, and all of a sudden you understand that your answer matters a great deal, that even though you do not know who is asking you the question you know for sure whom you are answering—well, go ahead and give it a try. You may say something stupid, but then again you may surprise yourself and say something inspired instead. The important thing is to *try*— not only to say what we believe but also to *live* what we believe—knowing that we are Peter's kin, and that whether we rise or whether we fall, whether we give the right answer or the wrong one, we too are chips off the old block, pieces of the one true rock against which even the very powers of death shall not prevail.

11

Risking Life

Matthew 16:21–27

From that time Jesus began to show his disciples that he must go to Jerusalem and suffer many things from the elders and chief priests and scribes, and be killed, and on the third day be raised. And Peter took him and began to rebuke him, saying, "God forbid, Lord! This shall never happen to you." But he turned and said to Peter, "Get behind me, Satan! You are a hindrance to me; for you are not on the side of God, but of men."

Then Jesus told his disciples, "If any man would come after me, let him deny himself and take up his cross and follow me. For whoever would save his life will lose it, and whoever loses his life for my sake will find it. For what will it profit a man, if he gains the whole world and forfeits his life? Or what shall a man give in return for his life? For the Son of man is to come with his angels in the glory of his Father, and then he will repay every man for what he has done."

This passage from the Gospel according to Matthew contains one of Jesus' hardest sayings. "If any man would come after me," he says to his disciples, "let him deny himself and take up his cross and follow me." It is one of those passages most of us could do without. We prefer passages like "Come to me, all ye who labor and are heavy laden, and I will give you rest" (Matt. 11:28), or "God so loved the world that he gave his only Son, that whoever believes in him should not perish but have eternal life" (John 3:16). Those are comfortable passages, safe passages, passages that provide some cushion in a sharp and often frightening world.

But "deny yourself and take up your cross"? Who needs that, when it is hard enough just to keep the bills paid and food on the table, when it is hard enough just to get up in the morning and face the challenges of an ordinary day? Some of us like to believe that Jesus was talking only to his disciples—those twelve special Christians—and that the rest of us are excused from denying ourselves and lugging crosses and things like that. Others of us insist that Jesus is the only one called to die on a cross, and that because he did, the rest of us do not have to.

Then again, we all know people who have taken this hard saying and made it their life's motto. They put themselves down all the time and shun comfort as if it were poisonous to their souls. They deny themselves the smallest pleasures of life and treat themselves like prisoners on death row, as if simple human happiness were some kind of disloyalty to God. Surely that cannot be what this passage is about; surely Jesus does not mean that the only way we can follow him is to take every shortcut to our own graves, but if he does not mean that, what *does* he mean? Do we really have to die for love of him? Isn't there some way to love him and *live*?

The whole conversation came about because Peter was asking the same questions. The disciples were off by themselves with Jesus, taking a breather between rounds with their critics. In the passage just before this one, Jesus asked his disciples who they thought he really was, and Peter gave the right answer. "You are the Christ," he said, "the Son of the living God," and Jesus rewarded Peter by calling him a rock, the rock on which Jesus would build his church.

But Peter's glory does not last long, because as soon as Jesus begins to tell his disciples what is about to be required of him, how he is about to walk right into the trap set for him in Jerusalem, where he will suffer, and be killed, and be raised from the dead, Peter explodes. "God forbid, Lord!" he says. "This shall never happen to you." It is simply too much for him, to imagine his wise, young teacher coming to such a quick and bloody end, especially an end that can be avoided. Why walk into a trap when you can turn around and walk away? Why take a risk you do not have to take?

Have you ever known someone who was headed that way? The newspaper occasionally runs stories about them: the man who rushes into the burning building to see if anyone has been left inside; the woman who dives into the hole in the frozen lake to rescue a child who has fallen through. Those are the dramatic stories, but there are quiet ones too: the doctor who spends several nights a week in a rundown part of town, giving free medical care to homeless men; the student who spends Saturday afternoons rocking babies with AIDS; the teacher who quits her job and spends all her savings to go teach Nicaraguan peasants how to read.

It is only human to admire such people, but there is an equally human part of us that is taken aback by them and afraid for them. We listen to the dangerous things they do or are planning to do and part of us, like Peter, wants to protest. "God forbid!" comes a voice from deep down inside us somewhere. "Isn't there an easier way to do what you want to do? Do you have to take such risks? What if you get hurt? What if you get killed? God forbid that something like that should happen to you!"

That is, in so many words, what Peter says to Jesus, and right or wrong, he has a way of saying what the rest of us are thinking. Over and over again he is the disciples' spokesman, the one who says the things they do not dare to say, the one who asks the questions they do not dare to ask. "God forbid, Lord!" he says when Jesus predicts his own death, and Jesus explodes.

"Get behind me, Satan!" he says to Peter. "You are a hindrance to me; for you are not on the side of God, but of men." What a shock that must have been for the other disciples, to hear Peter, the first disciple, called Satan; to hear Peter, the foundation rock of the church, called a hindrance, a stumbling block, in Jesus' path. What did he do wrong? What was his sin? All he did was protest the forecast that Jesus would suffer and die. All he did was say out loud that there had to be another way.

But as far as Jesus was concerned, it was Satan talking. Satan, the ancient tempter, from the beginning of time has offered humankind alternatives to the will of God—easier alternatives, safer alternatives, flashier alternatives—all of them temptations for us to do and be something other than what God has called us to do and be. In the case at hand, the temptation for Jesus is to play things safe, to skip the trip to Jerusalem and find another way to save the world—to direct the effort from secret headquarters, to elude his enemies, staying just out of their reach and leading his holy revolution without placing himself at risk.

We must assume that it is a real temptation for Jesus, or else why does he silence Peter so harshly? Like the tempter in the wilderness, Peter is offering him a way out, a detour around Jerusalem with all its risk of pain and death, and for a moment, perhaps, the possibility seems real to Jesus, real and to be desired, before his head clears and the dream vanishes. "Get behind me, Satan!" he says, however tempted he may be, "for you are not on the side of God but of men."

Here is what really troubles me about that: Does Jesus mean that all of us who pray to be delivered from suffering and death are on the side of men, and that the side of God is reserved only for those who are ready and willing to die? Does he mean that all of us who want to be on God's side had better go out and get ourselves killed as soon as possible? That troubles me! I want to believe that God *gives* me my life, not that God is eager to take it away. I want to believe that God wills my survival, not that God is looking forward to my funeral. Doesn't God want me to be happy? Doesn't God care about my comfort and safety?

The resounding answer, according to this morning's passage, is "No!" God does not care about my comfort and safety. God does not care whether I am happy or not. What God cares about, with all the power of God's holy being, is the *quality* of my life. Not just my life, mind you, not just the continuation of my breath and the health of my cells, but the quality of my life—the depth of my life, the scope of my life, the heft and zest of my life.

The deep secret of Jesus' hard words to us in this passage is that our fear of suffering and death robs us of life, because fear of death always turns into fear of life, into a stingy, cautious way of living that is not really living at all. The deep secret of Jesus' hard words is that the way to have abundant life is not to save it but to spend it, to give it away, because life cannot be shut up and saved any more than a bird can be put in a shoebox and stored on a closet shelf.

Better yet, life cannot be shut up and saved any more than fresh spring water can be put in a mason jar and kept in a kitchen cupboard. It will remain water, and if you ever open it up you can probably still drink it, but it will have lost its essence, its life, which is to be poured out, to be moving, living water, rushing downstream to share its wealth without ever looking back.

Peter wanted to prevent Jesus from doing that. He did not want Jesus' life to be spilled, to be wasted. He wanted to save it, to preserve it, to find a safer, more comfortable way for Jesus to be Lord. What he forgot, apparently, was that Jesus' supply of life was never-ending, that what poured out of him poured out of an underground source so fine, so strong, that the more of himself he gave, the more he had—a veritable geyser of living water sent to drench a dry, dry world.

Peter missed that part of what Jesus said, but so did I, the first nine or ten times I heard it. Listen again to what Matthew says: "Jesus began to show his disciples that he must go to Jerusalem and suffer many things from the elders and chief priests and scribes, and be killed, and on the third day be raised." *And on the third day be raised.* Peter missed that part and so did I. We never got that far. We got stuck on the suffering and death part. We got that far and said, "God forbid, Lord! This shall never happen to you," without finishing the sentence, without noticing that after the suffering and death part there is life again, abundant life, life for Jesus and for all of us that can never be cut off.

You just never get that far if you let suffering and death

throw you off the track, if you let your fear of those things keep you from sticking your neck out, from taking the risks that make life worth living. You can try to save your own life. You can try to stockpile it, being very, very careful about what you say yes to; being very, very cautious about whom you let into your life, frisking everyone at the door and letting only the most harmless people inside; and being very, very wary about going outside yourself, venturing forth only under very heavy guard and ready to retreat at the first sign of trouble.

You can live that way, but do not expect to enjoy it very much, or to accomplish very much, and do not expect to be missed when your safe, comfortable life finally comes to an end and no one notices that you are gone. "For whoever would save his life will lose it," Jesus says to his disciples, "and whoever loses his life for my sake will find it."

Living the life of faith is not about being a daredevil, in other words. This is not a sermon about signing up for skydiving lessons or doing dangerous things for the thrill of it. This is a sermon about living a life that matters—a life for Christ's sake—and about refusing to put our own comfort and safety ahead of living a life like that, a life that pours itself out for others as a matter of course, a life that spends itself without counting the cost, knowing that there is always more life where our own life comes from, and that even when our own lives run out God will have more life in store for us, because our God is a God who never runs out of life.

"If any man would come after me," Jesus says, "let him deny himself and take up his cross and follow me." Those will never be easy words to hear, but they are not, in the final analysis, an invitation to follow Jesus into death but an invitation to follow him into life, both now and later on. We can only follow him, however, if we do not get tripped up on suffering and death, if we do not get so frightened and preoccupied by those that we forget who we are and whose we are and why we are alive in the first place.

There is a certain amount of pain involved in being human, and a good bit more involved in being fully human, fully alive, especially in a world that counts on our fear of death and uses it to keep us in line. Jesus' enemies counted on his fear of death to shut him up and shut him down, but they were wrong. He may have been afraid, but he did not let his fear stop him. He did not get stuck on the suffering and death part. He saw something beyond them, something as wide and glittering as the sea, worth every risk required to reach it, and he did not stop until he got there.

To be where God is—to follow Jesus—means going beyond the limits of our own comfort and safety. It means receiving our lives as gifts instead of guarding them as our own possessions. It means sharing the life we have been given instead of bottling it for our own consumption. It means giving up the notion that we can build dams to contain the bright streams of our lives and letting them go instead, letting them swell their banks and spill their wealth until they carry us down to where they run, full and growing fuller, into the wide and glittering sea.

12

Family Fights

Matthew 18:15–20

Jesus said, "If your brother sins against you, go and tell
him his fault, between you and him alone. If he listens to
you, you have gained your brother. But if he does not listen, take one or two others along with you, that every
word may be confirmed by the evidence of two or three
witnesses. If he refuses to listen to them, tell it to the
church; and if he refuses to listen even to the church, let
him be to you as a Gentile and a tax collector. Truly, I say
to you, whatever you bind on earth shall be bound in
heaven, and whatever you loose on earth shall be loosed in
heaven. Again I say to you, if two of you agree on earth
about anything they ask, it will be done for them by my
Father in heaven. For where two or three are gathered in
my name, there am I in the midst of them."

Throughout the eighteenth chapter of Matthew, and in these
six verses in particular, Jesus underscores the importance of
Christian community. Speaking to his disciples, he lets them
know that their faith is not a private matter, something they can
go off by themselves and enjoy all alone under a tree. Their life
in Christ is a community affair, something that happens when
two or three of them are gathered together in his name. *That* is

when he promises to be in their midst, and not when they are off by themselves feeling holy.

He lets them know that they need each other, in other words—not only for practical reasons but for spiritual ones as well. They need each other because two heads are better than one; they need each other because they can accomplish more together than they can apart. They need each other like brothers and sisters need each other, to remind themselves that they belong to one family.

When families work right, they are God's way of teaching us important things, like how to share and how to work together and how to take care of one another. A healthy family has a way of smoothing our rough edges by making us rub up against each other, like tumbling pebbles in a jar. Living with other people, we learn that we cannot have everything our own way. We learn to compromise, giving up some of the things we want so that other people can have some of the things they want, and while it is never easy, learning this give and take is part of learning how to be fully human.

Another thing that living in a family can teach you is how to fight, especially if you have brothers and sisters to practice on. I am the eldest of three daughters who practiced a lot, two of us ganging up on the third in alliances that were always shifting. We wrestled, we argued, we slammed doors and pulled pigtails. Sometimes we stopped speaking to one another and the silence would go on for hours, which made it difficult to continue the fight.

One night over dinner I discovered an excellent way to use the silence, however. I must have been about eleven at the time, which means that my youngest sister, Jennifer, was five. My technique was this: While my mother was busy putting food on the table and my father had not yet figured out what was going on, I fixed my little sister with a terrible stare, narrowing my eyes and glaring at her as I breathed heavier and heavier, doing my best impression of a crazed killer.

It worked. Poor Jenny was terrified, but could find no words to describe what I was doing to her, until finally she burst into tears, crying, "Daddy, make her stop breathing! She's *breathing* at me!" Seeing what I had done, I leapt up from my chair and ran to comfort her, telling her that I would not breathe at her anymore. We knew how to fight, but we also knew how to make up, forgetting our differences and forgiving each other for the mean things we sometimes did.

Not everyone has such memories of growing up, however, because many families do *not* work right. They are not schools in forbearance and forgiveness but reformatories where rules are more important than people and where the first rule is silence, silence about anything unpleasant or untoward. If you cannot say something nice do not say anything at all, and if you have a problem with someone, keep it to yourself, because harmony—even the *illusion* of harmony—is the most important thing, more important than telling the truth, more important than your feelings, and more important, finally, than you.

That is the lesson many families teach and it is a crying shame, but in today's reading Jesus lets us know that the Christian family does not work that way, that in the household of God, when your brother sins against you, you must go and talk to him, and if that does not work you must keep going back— taking other people with you next time—doing everything in your power to get your brother back again.

There are two curious things about Jesus' advice. First, he puts the burden on the *victim*, on the person who has been sinned *against*. Second, he seems much less interested in who is right and who is wrong than he is in getting the family back together again. The important thing is that we listen to each other, he says, but if a member of the family refuses to listen over and over again—if the doors to communication stay firmly shut—then we are not to pretend that nothing has happened. We are to recognize that one of our members has left the family, because the only thing worse than losing a brother or sister is pretending that you have not and letting that person fester in your midst like an untended wound.

It is hard but honest advice, one of those pieces of advice that we know is right, that we know we should take, but one that is very hard to act upon. Can you imagine doing exactly as Jesus suggests? If you do not belong to a church community, suppose for a moment that you do—a neighborhood church, say, of about two hundred and fifty members. Week after week you sit in a pew next to Joe, whom you get to know rather well, so well that one day in early September he asks if he can borrow your lawn mower.

Sure, you say, full of good Christian cheer, and Joe assures you that he will bring it back within the week. But the week passes, and then another week, until finally you call Joe and ask him if you can have your lawn mower back, which is when he tells you that he has loaned it to someone else who has backed over it in his truck and that the lawn mower is no more. Joe considers this a piece of bad luck that the two of you share, but you consider that you have been wronged.

So the first thing you do is to go over to Joe's by yourself and talk it over with him, offering to take half of what the lawn mower was worth for the sake of the friendship, but Joe is offended. Can he help it if the guy ran over the lawn mower with his truck? He says that these things happen, and he is sorry it happened to you, but that does not make it his fault. So you go home, open the church directory at random, and call the first two names you see, asking them to go back to Joe's with you and help you work things out with him.

Next day after work the three of you knock on Joe's door. He is surprised to see you and gets mad when you tell him why you are there. What are you trying to do, gang up on him? Drag his name through the mud? Standing there on the porch, you start to tell him that you have reconsidered, that you are willing to report the loss of the lawn mower to your insurance company if Joe will just tell them what happened, but before you can finish your speech Joe tells you to get off his property before he calls the police, and then he shuts the door in your face.

What do you do next? You guessed it: You call everyone in the church and ask them to meet you at Joe's house next Saturday morning. Since you doubt that he will answer the door, you make signs he can read through his windows, signs that say, "Forget the lawn mower, Joe" and "We are your friends" or "Come out and talk." On Saturday everyone is there, milling around on Joe's front lawn, carrying their signs and watching the house, which is as dark and still as a tomb. Nothing happens for twenty minutes or so, but then you see one slat of the venetian blinds pulled back, and while you cannot see Joe you know that he can see you, so you wave and smile and beckon to him to come out. Then the slat pops back into place and nothing happens for another twenty minutes, until you look up and see Joe standing sheepishly on his front porch, a check for the lawn mower in his hand. The crowd cheers, you and Joe embrace, and everyone lives happily ever after. The End.

I know what you are thinking. "Maybe so and maybe not," you are thinking, but how would we know? I have never tried anything like that, have you? When someone crosses me, my strategies are usually quite different, and my hunch is that yours are too. The first one, the one that comes most naturally, is to pretend that nothing has happened. Forget the lawn mower. Just let it go. No need to get upset. Maybe he will bring it back someday; maybe you will not have to ask. Meanwhile, it is awkward to be around him, but that is better than a fight. Ignore it and it will go away, or at least you will not have to think about it as much.

A second strategy is the cold shoulder. You never tell the other person what is wrong because that would be impolite, so you just shun the offender—not only Joe but anyone who does something you do not like. You simply X them out of your mind, and when you walk past them it is like no one is there. It never occurs to you to ask them about what really happened between the two of you because you are sure you already know. *They* were in the wrong; let *them* figure it out.

Yet a third strategy is revenge—the silent, deadly kind—where you never admit any ill will toward someone but you let it leak out all over the place, never missing an opportunity to question the other person's character or tell a little joke at his expense. You embark on a private smear campaign, telling yourself that it makes you feel better, telling yourself that over and over and over again because the truth is that you do not really feel any better at all.

In his book *The Great Divorce*, the British writer C. S. Lewis paints a picture of hell that haunts me, because it bears such resemblance to where many human beings live. Hell is like a vast, gray city, Lewis says, a city inhabited only at its outer edges, with rows and rows of empty houses in the middle—empty because everyone who once lived in them has quarreled with the neighbors and moved, and quarreled with the new neighbors and moved again, leaving empty streets full of empty houses behind them. That, Lewis says, is how hell got so large—empty at the center and inhabited only on the fringes—because everyone in it chose distance instead of confrontation as the solution to a fight.

By confrontation I mean just what the dictionary says: to bring two people face to face, front to front, to sort out what is going on between them. That is what today's reading recommends, and it is also what most of us would do just about anything to avoid. The excuses rush to our lips. Who am I to judge? What is it to me? *I* go to *her*? *She* is the sinner; let *her* come to *me*. *Tell* him my feelings are hurt? What if he just hurts them again? I would not know what to say. I would feel so foolish. And what is the use, anyhow? Things will never change.

Those are all fine excuses, if you do not mind living on the outskirts of hell, but for those of us who are called to Christian community, they just will not do. For us, there is something more important than being right or wrong, and that something is keeping the family together. For us the real problem is not the brother or sister who sins against us but our own fierce wish to defend ourselves against them regardless of the cost. The real problem is the speed with which most of us are ready to forsake our relationships in favor of nursing our hurt feelings, our wounded pride. In old-fashioned language, the problem is how eager we are to repay sin with more sin.

There is another way, apparently, an alternative to putting distance between ourselves and those with whom we are in conflict. We can go to them, Jesus says, and tell them what is wrong, or what we think is wrong, because the best way to end a fight is to admit that we too might be wrong. There are certain questions to be asked, such as: Am I sure I know what I am talking about? Have I given the other person every benefit of the doubt? What are my motives in confronting her with my feelings? Do I want to make him feel bad, or do I really want peace? What am I afraid of? Is the relationship worth the risk?

That last question is a very important one, because the only reason to take Jesus' advice at all is to win back a relationship that is in danger of being lost. Once you have decided that is what you want, it helps to remember that you are working *for* the relationship, not *against* it; that your goal is *reconciliation*, not *retribution*; and that being right is less important to you than being in relationship.

Assuming you have made it this far, you are now ready for the final step, which is setting the lunch date, making the telephone call, or writing the letter that will halt the spread of hell. If this is not something you are eager to do, do not let that stop you; there is not a word in today's reading about wanting to reach out to your brother or sister. Just go, it says, and try to gain the relationship back.

In a lot of ways, it is a real nuisance to belong to a family. It would be so much easier if we were just a bunch of individuals, loosely bound by similar beliefs but whose affairs remained an essentially private matter between us and God. But according to Jesus, there is no such thing as privacy in the family of God. Our life together is the chief means God has chosen for being with us, and it is of ultimate importance to God. Our life together is the place where we are comforted, confronted, tested, and redeemed by God through one another. It is the place where we come to know God or to flee from God's presence, depending upon how we come to know or flee from one another.

When someone crosses us, we are called to be the first to reach out, even when we are the ones who have been hurt, even when God knows we have done nothing wrong, even when everything in us wants to fight back—still we are called to community with one another, to act like the family we are. That is how we know God and how God knows us. That is what we are called to do: to confront and make up, to forgive and seek forgiveness, to heal and be healed—to throw a block party smack in the deserted center of hell and fill the place with such music and laughter, such merriment and mutual affection that all the far-flung residents come creeping in from their distant outposts to see what the fuss, the light, the *joy* is all about.

13

Once More from the Heart

Matthew 18:21–35

Then Peter came up and said to him, "Lord, how often shall my brother sin against me, and I forgive him? As many as seven times?" Jesus said to him, "I do not say to you seven times, but seventy times seven.

"Therefore the kingdom of heaven may be compared to a king who wished to settle accounts with his servants. When he began the reckoning, one was brought to him who owed him ten thousand talents; and as he could not pay, his lord ordered him to be sold, with his wife and children and all that he had, and payment to be made. So the servant fell on his knees, imploring him, 'Lord, have patience with me, and I will pay you everything.' And out of pity for him the lord of that servant released him and forgave him the debt. But that same servant, as he went out, came upon one of his fellow servants who owed him a hundred denarii; and seizing him by the throat he said, 'Pay what you owe.' So his fellow servant fell down and besought him, 'Have patience with me, and I will pay you.' He refused and went and put him in prison till he should pay the debt. When his fellow servants saw what had taken place, they were greatly distressed, and they went and reported to their lord all that had taken place. Then his lord summoned him and said to him, 'You wicked servant! I forgave you all that debt because you besought me; and should not you have had mercy on your fellow servant, as I had mercy on you?' And in anger his lord delivered him to the jailers, till he should pay all his debt. So also my heavenly Father will do to every one of you, if you do not forgive your brother from your heart."

This parable of the Wicked Servant is a prickly one. It ends the section of Matthew's Gospel in which Jesus talks at length about what relationships in the Christian community are like, a section in which he makes the same point over and over again: that the life of the community—the family of God—is the most important thing in the world, and that those who want to be members of it are called to do everything in their power to nourish and strengthen the bonds of their love.

Nothing is to get in the way of that, not their quarrels with one another, not their rivalries, not their tendency to put each other down, not even their blatant sins. If one of them goes astray, they are to leave the rest of the flock and go find the lost one; if one of them does wrong and separates himself from the community, they are to go and try to bring him back.

Listening to Jesus go on in this vein, the disciple Peter becomes concerned about what, exactly, is required of him. He is looking for a guideline, a limit to how far he must go with this relationship business. "Lord," he asks Jesus, "how often shall my brother sin against me, and I forgive him? As many as seven times?" he says, no doubt thinking that seven is a *lot* of times, more times than most people can forgive anyone, but he gets no credit for his generous suggestion.

"I do not say to you seven times," Jesus replies, "but seventy times seven," which is about the same as saying that there is no limit to forgiveness, that forgiving those who sin against us is not something we ever get done with but something that goes on forever; that it is not a favor we bestow seven times and withhold the eighth, but a way of life that never ends.

If you really think about that, it can wear you out. Forgiving someone once can be strenuous enough. Say you have a lunch date with a friend that you go to a lot of trouble to keep. You leave early enough so that you will be there on time, and even though you have to circle the block five times to find a parking place, you make it, choosing a nice table near the window and settling down to wait—and wait, and wait, and wait—until it becomes clear that you have been stood up, and you pay your check and leave, telling yourself that your friend had better have a good excuse.

Later that afternoon she calls, saying how stupid she feels, that she left her appointment book at home and did not remember until just that minute that the two of you had a lunch date. She is so sorry, she says; will you give her another chance? You put your feelings aside. Of course you will; what is one missed lunch between friends? So you set another date, and the day arrives, and the whole thing happens all over again. Forgiving someone once is one thing, but are you really going to set another lunch date? Are you really willing to go through this routine seventy times seven, or to be more specific, four hundred and eighty-eight more times?

Not likely. Human nature does not work that way. Most of us are willing to get burned once, a lot of us even twice, but the third time we tend to back off. It is as if we have little calculators in our heads, keeping track of how much we are putting *into* our relationships versus how much we are getting *out* of them, and not many of us pursue those with a negative balance. When someone lets us down again and again, we tend to turn our attention elsewhere. We prefer cost-efficient relationships in which there is a better rate of exchange, in which what we *give* and what we *get* are more nearly even. That may be a crass way to put it, but you know it is true. No one wants a one-way relationship, in which one person does all the giving while the other one just gets and gets and gets.

That is the part of us that Jesus is speaking to in today's reading, the part of us that—like Peter—wants to place a limit on our involvement with people who run up debts with us. We try to be patient. We try to stay open to them, but surely there is a limit. Isn't seven times enough? After we have forgiven them seven times and been taken advantage of every time, isn't that enough? Can't we stop and find something else to do for a change?

As is his custom, Jesus answers Peter's question with a story, a story about a king who wishes to settle accounts with his servants, many of whom owe him money. He is a king who keeps good books, who employs several accountants to keep track of who owes him what, and several jailers as well, to lock up those who cannot pay. On this particular day of reckoning he apparently starts at the top of the list, because the first servant who is brought before him owes him an enormous sum—10,000 talents, Jesus says, a ridiculous amount—roughly 1.5 billion dollars by today's standards.

Clearly, the servant cannot pay that amount, so the king orders him and his family to be sold. The price they will bring will not begin to cover their debt, but the king is in the business of cutting his losses, and selling the servant is less expensive than keeping him around. Realizing that the jig is up, the servant falls on his knees and promises to pay everything he owes if the king will just be patient.

It is an absurd promise. If he works forty hours a week for the next 150,000 years he will never be able to pay what he owes, but the king is moved, both by the servant's plight and by his plea, so he has pity on him and releases him, forgiving him his debt. He goes out of the bookkeeping business, at least as far as this servant is concerned. He accepts the risk of remaining in relationship with him. For reasons known only to himself, he cancels his servant's debt and gives him back his life again, out of the goodness of his royal heart.

Within moments, the servant has a chance to return the favor by forgiving one of his own debtors, a man who owes him 100 denarii—or about three thousand dollars—but that apparently never occurs to him. Instead, he grabs the man by the throat, demanding his due, and when the man says the same thing to *him* that *he* said to the *king*—"Have patience with me and I will pay you"—he has the man thrown into jail.

The king gets wind of what he has done and does the same thing to him, revoking the mercy he showed before and sentencing his servant to life in prison. "You wicked servant!" he says to him. "I forgave you all that debt because you besought me; and should you not have had mercy on your fellow servant as I had mercy on you?"

I told you it was a prickly parable. On the surface, it is a lesson about the Golden Rule: Do unto others as you would have them do unto you. Or to put it more bluntly: Do unto others as you would have *God* do unto you, because if you do not forgive your brother from your heart your heavenly Father will have you hauled off to jail and throw away the key.

Frankly, I think that is a terrible reading of the parable. If the only reason to forgive my neighbor is to save my own neck, to secure my own forgiveness, then it is not something I am doing out of love but out of fear, and does that sound like Jesus to you? It does not sound like Jesus to me, which makes me think that we have got to look below the surface to discover what this parable is all about. How did this story start out so well and end so poorly? What went wrong? What made the servant so wicked, so unable to forgive a mere fraction of the debt that he himself had just been forgiven?

When I think about my own understanding of forgiveness, it is clear that I am a student of my own experience. If I am able to forgive at all, it is because I have been forgiven, because thanks to someone else, I know how it feels to have my debts cancelled, my credit restored, my relationship renewed. When it has happened to me, it is like someone has taken a big pink eraser and scrubbed my record clean, or better yet, has retired the ledger with my name on it and refused to keep score anymore. It is an incredible experience, but it is never one of my own doing. All I have ever been able to do is ask for it—to ask for forgiveness—but when it has been granted it has come to me from outside myself, a free gift from someone whom I have hurt, whom I have owed, but who has decided that what is more important than getting even is to remain in relationship with me.

That is, as best I can say it, what real forgiveness is all about: pure, unadulterated grace. But anyone who has experienced the genuine article knows that there are also a lot of impostors around. People overlook one another's faults or make excuses for them and call it forgiveness. They hide their feelings in order to avoid a fight and call it forgiveness. They learn how to say things that sound forgiving and call it forgiveness, while their actions bear no resemblance to their words.

There is a lot that passes for forgiveness these days that is not forgiveness at all but a kind of indifference, in which we dismiss people from our lives by "forgiving" them and then have less and less to do with them until finally there is nothing left between us at all.

When that happens, the only excuse I can think of is that we have forgotten what it is like to be forgiven, genuinely forgiven from the heart, because if we could remember what that is really like, how could we deprive anyone else of the same experience? It would be like refusing to share food or water, like breathing in and refusing to breathe out. Once we have experienced the exhilaration of real forgiveness, how could we fail to pass it on?

That is what the king wants to know. "I remitted the whole of your debt when you appealed to me," he says to his wicked servant. "Were you not bound to show your fellow servant the same pity as I showed you?" (NEB). The king who quit keeping score on his servant wants to know why his servant could not do the same thing, and all I can figure is that the servant missed the significance of what had happened to him.

Somehow, when the king released him and forgave him his debt, he did not get it. He thought he had gotten away with something. He thought he had pulled a fast one. He thought the king was soft in the head to buy such an obvious lie. "Lord, have patience with me and I will pay you everything." He could *never* repay what he owed. He knew it and the king knew it, but if making the king feel sorry for him meant he did not have to pay, what did he care?

He missed the experience of forgiveness altogether. It never occurred to him that he was not being let off the hook, or being patronized by a sentimental old monarch. It never crossed his mind that what was *really* happening to him was that he was being forgiven from the heart by someone who understood the enormity of his debt—indeed, by someone who had financed it—but who was willing to let it all go, to stop keeping score, to erase the debt that had become a substitute for the relationship so that they could get to know one another again.

That is what real forgiveness is all about. The only reason for any of us ever to forgive each other is because we want the relationship back again, which is hard to do when you are keeping score. As long as you are focused on what someone owes you, you tend to spend your time figuring out how to get paid back, or proved right, or protected from further harm. But once you have forgiven your brother or sister from your heart, there is all the time in the world—time to put the calculator away and go for a walk, time to compare notes on what you have learned, time to get to know one another again.

That is what the wicked servant missed. When the king forgave him, he just figured that he had outsmarted the old guy, and that the best way to cut his own losses was to see that the same thing did not happen to him. So when his turn came, he did what he had fully expected the king to do to him: He grabbed his debtor by the throat and demanded to be paid. He had missed his own forgiveness, so of course he could not forgive anyone else. All he saw when he looked at his fellow servant was an overdue bill walking around, and he grabbed it by the throat.

You know how it ends. He gets thrown in jail until he can pay his debt, which amounts to the rest of his life, but his imprisonment is a technicality. The wicked servant was *already* behind bars, bars of his own making. By refusing to be forgiven and refusing to forgive, he had already created his own little Alcatraz, where he sat in solitary confinement with his calculator and kept track of his accounts.

"Lord, how often shall my brother sin against me, and I forgive him?" Peter says. "As many as seven times?"

"I do not say to you seven times," Jesus replies, "but seventy times seven."

By the end of the parable, Peter thinks he has gotten the message: Do unto others or the king will do unto you—only that is not the message of the parable at all. The message of the parable is: Do unto others as the king has *already* done unto you. It is not a matter of earning your forgiveness, or letting others off the hook so that you will be let off the hook yourself.

It is a matter of understanding that you have *already* been forgiven, that someone to whom you owe everything—your life and breath, your blue eyes, your fondness for fresh tomatoes, your pleasure in the moon and stars, all the loves of your life—someone who has given and given and given to you and who has gotten precious little in return has examined your enormous debt in great detail and knows from your credit rating that the chances of repayment are nil. Someone who knows all of that has taken the stack of your IOUs and torn them in two, balancing your books in one fell swoop for one reason and one reason alone: because that someone wants to remain in relationship with you, and wants you to be free to respond.

When someone like that has stopped keeping score on you, you feel sort of foolish keeping score on the people in your own life. You feel sort of petty, wanting to write them off after seven times, or even after seventy times seven, for that matter, when you consider how many times you have been forgiven yourself, forgiven from the heart over and over and over again, through no merit of your own but simply because someone loves you very, very much and wants to love you some more. Once you have let that sink in, once you have really taken that into your own heart, how can you—how can any of us—pass up a single chance to do the same?

14

Beginning at the End

Matthew 20:1–16

Jesus said, "The kingdom of heaven is like a householder who went out early in the morning to hire laborers for his vineyard. After agreeing with the laborers for a denarius a day, he sent them into his vineyard. And going out about the third hour he saw others standing idle in the market-place; and to them he said, 'You go into the vineyard too, and whatever is right I will give you.' So they went. Going out again about the sixth hour and the ninth hour, he did the same. And about the eleventh hour he went out and found others standing; and he said to them, 'Why do you stand here idle all day?' They said to him, 'Because no one has hired us.' He said to them, 'You go into the vineyard too.' And when evening came, the owner of the vineyard said to his steward, 'Call the laborers and pay them their wages, beginning with the last, up to the first.' And when those hired about the eleventh hour came, each of them received a denarius. Now when the first came, they thought they would receive more; but each of them also received a denarius. And on receiving it they grumbled at the householder, saying, 'These last worked only one hour, and you have made them equal to us who have borne the burden of the day and the scorching heat.' But he replied to one of them, 'Friend, I am doing you no wrong;

did you not agree with me for a denarius? Take what belongs to you, and go; I choose to give to this last as I give to you. Am I not allowed to do what I choose with what belongs to me? Or do you begrudge my generosity?' So the last will be first, and the first last."

The parable of the Laborers in the Vineyard is a little like cod liver oil: You know Jesus is right, you know it must be good for you, but that does not make it any easier to swallow. Along with the parable of the Prodigal Son, today's parable is one of those stories of forgiveness so radical that it offends, because it seems to reward those who have done the least while it sends those who have worked the hardest to the end of the line.

"So the last will be first and the first last," Jesus says, scrambling the usual order of things, challenging the sacred assumption by which most of us live our lives, namely, that the front of the line is the place to be, that the way to win God's attention is to be the best person, the hardest worker, the first one into the vineyard in the morning and the last one to leave at night. Only according to today's reading, where that will get you is exactly nowhere. According to the parable of the Laborers in the Vineyard, those at the end of the line will not only be paid as much as those at the front; they will also be paid *first*. It is just not fair.

One thing that often helps me understand hard stories like this one is to see where they fit. At what point in his life does Jesus tell the story? Where is he and what is he doing? To whom is he talking? What has just happened and what happens next?

If you turn to the nineteenth chapter of Matthew, for instance, to the paragraph just before this parable, you find out that Peter has just asked Jesus what he and the other disciples can expect in the way of reward for their loyalty to Jesus. They have given up everything to follow him, Peter points out. What will he give them in return? Jesus promises them twelve thrones in the world to come. "But many that are first will be last," he says, "and the last first." Then he tells the parable of the Laborers in the Vineyard.

That is what happens *before* the story. What happens *after* it is that James and John's mother comes up to Jesus and makes a special case for her two sons, asking Jesus to give them the best thrones in the kingdom, one on his left and one on his right. Politely but firmly, Jesus lets her know that she doesn't know what she is talking about, because his throne will not be made out of gold and jewels but out of wood and nails, in the shape of a cross.

It helps to know where the parable fits, that both before and after Jesus tells it, his own disciples are jockeying for position, wanting good seats in the kingdom, competing for the best seats, each of them trying to be first in line when the doors are propped open and the show begins.

Have you ever done that? I remember waiting in line for the Saturday afternoon matinee at the local movie theatre when I was a little girl. It was summertime, and there were always lots of us there. Our parents would drop us off in the heat of the afternoon, giddy at the prospect of a couple hours' peace and quiet. We stood in the shade of the awning outside and waited for the box office to open, our dollar bills burning holes in our pockets as we debated the economics of popcorn versus Junior Mints or Milk Duds.

We were loud and boisterous, standing so close together that we could smell each other—that damp, healthy smell that children give off in the summertime. Our friends would arrive and we would shout their names, motioning them over to claim the places we had saved for them. The children behind us would complain bitterly and so would we when the same thing happened in front of us, but it was all part of the game.

Where every one of us wanted to be was right up there at the front of the line. That was the best place to be, not only because you were the first inside, but because you were there when the moment came, when the doors were unlocked, and the timid-looking manager pushed them open, so that a great wave of cold air rolled out of the dark theatre and hit you like a blast from the Arctic, an icy promise of everything that waited for you inside. That was the moment everyone waited for, and those who had won places at the front of the line got the very best of it.

I cannot imagine anything more disheartening than if the manager had come outside and reversed the order, telling those of us at the front of the line to stay put while he invited those at the end of the line—those who had just arrived, those who were not even hot yet from standing in the sun—while he invited them to enter the theatre first. I think I would have cried; I certainly would have booed, because it would not have been fair. Those of us at the front of the line had *earned* our reward; we knew it and so did everyone else. On what grounds would anyone dare reverse the order?

According to today's story, the manager just feels like being generous. Those are his grounds. He can do whatever he wants to do in his own vineyard, and what he wants is to let the last be first and the first be last. Everyone will be paid; no one will go home empty handed. He simply wants to reverse the order and pay all the workers the same thing, regardless of how long they have stood in the sun.

Some of them have been there since dawn, mind you. Early that morning the householder went to the marketplace, to the corner where those without steady jobs hung out, and he hired a handful of them to work in his vineyard for the day. He offered them a denarius—a fair day's wage—and they agreed, but by nine in the morning it was clear there was more work than they could do. So the householder went back to the corner again, and again at noon, and again at three in the afternoon, bringing more workers back with him each time after promising to pay them whatever was right.

Finally, at five in the afternoon, with only one hour left before dark, he goes back to the corner and finds a few men still standing idle. Rounding them up, he takes them back to the vineyard, where they help the others finish up the day's work. Then comes the moment they have all been waiting for. The blazing sun goes down, a cool breeze stirs the dusk, and the householder calls his steward to give them all their pay.

Beginning with the last to be hired, he presses a denarius into each of their hands. When they gasp out loud, the others strain to see and a murmur goes through the crowd. The householder has turned out to be a very generous man! If he pays the latecomers a whole denarius for just one hour's work, then those who arrived at dawn are about to be rich!

But before they can do the arithmetic in their heads, the steward has paid them all—one denarius. Whether they came at dawn and slaved all day or showed up at five to work the last hour, their pay is the same, and the murmurs at the front of the line quickly turn to grumbling. "These last worked only one hour, and you have made them equal to us," say the first to be hired, their faces all sunburned and their clothes sweated through. "You have made them equal to us who have borne the burden of the day and the scorching heat."

That is when the householder reminds them that he has kept his part of the bargain, that he has paid them exactly what they agreed to be paid, and what business is it of theirs what he pays the others? The vineyard is his, the money is his. Isn't he allowed to do what he wants to with what belongs to him? "Or do you," he says, "begrudge my generosity?"

You bet they do. Like most human beings, they have an innate sense of what is fair and what is not. Equal pay for equal work is fair; equal pay for unequal work is not fair. Rewarding those who do the most work is fair; rewarding those who do the least is not fair. Treating everyone the same is fair; treating everyone the same when they are *not* the same is not fair.

Life is so often not fair. You have heard the stories: A state employee arrives at her desk early every morning, answering the telephone until her tardy coworkers appear. She skips lunch in order to catch up on the filing and stays late to fill out reports for her supervisor, who has learned that she is the only one in the department who knows what is going on. When annual raises are due, he calls her into his office and explains that while she has done a superlative job, there will be no merit increases this year. Salaries will be increased across the board, with everyone receiving the same amount, because he thinks that will do more for group morale. It is not fair.

Or a man cares for his elderly mother, taking her into his own home when she becomes too frail to live by herself, and although he has three brothers and sisters, he rarely hears from them. They call from time to time to tell him how grateful they are, but none of them offers to help. "They have problems of their own," his mother tells him, patting his hand. "I just thank God for you." Then she dies and suddenly the whole family appears, grieving as if they had been there all along. At the lawyer's office they are all ears. The man who has spent most of his savings caring for his mother sits and listens with his head in his hands as the will is read. "I leave my estate to be divided equally among my four dear children," it reads, "because I love them all the same." It is just not fair.

Life is not fair, which is why it seems all that much more important that God should be. God should be the *one* authority whom you can count on to reward people according to their efforts, who keeps track of how long you have worked and how hard you have worked and who does not let people break into line ahead of you. God should be the *one* manager who polices the line, walking up and down to make sure everyone stays where he or she belongs, so that the first remain first and the last wait their turns at the end of the line. Life may not be fair, but God should be.

But it is not so, according to today's story. According to today's story, God is the householder who puts the same amount of money into a stack of little white envelopes and instructs his steward to pass them out beginning at the *end* of the line, with those who arrived last and worked least. Moving from that end of the line toward the front, where those who arrived first and worked most are standing, the steward does what he is told, but depending on where he is in the line the response he gets is quite different.

At the end of the line, with the last and the least, there is a lot of cheering, a lot of laughter and back slapping, while nearer the front, with the first and the most, there is loud grumbling and great hostility, so that the steward hands over the envelopes faster and faster, ready to run for his life. In every case, the pay is the same—a fair day's wage—but how it is received depends entirely on what each man believes he *deserves*. Those who have gotten more than they think they deserve are jubilant, while those who have gotten less are furious. "Take what belongs to you, and go," the householder tells them. "Am I not allowed to do what I choose with what belongs to me?"

The most curious thing about this parable for me is where we locate ourselves in line. The story sounds quite different from the end of the line, after all, than it does from the front of the line, but isn't it interesting that 99 percent of us hear it from front-row seats? *We* are the ones who have gotten the short end of the stick; *we* are the ones who have been cheated. *We* are the ones who have gotten up early and worked hard and stayed late and all for what? So that some backward householder can come along and start at the wrong end of the line, treating us just like the ne'er-do-wells who do not even get dressed until noon!

That is how most of us hear the parable, but it is entirely possible that we are mistaken about where we are in line. Did you ever think about that? It is entirely possible that, as far as God is concerned, we are halfway around the block, that there are all sorts of people ahead of us in line, people who are far more deserving of God's love than we are, people who have more stars in their crowns than we will ever have.

They are at the front of the line, and we are near the end of it for all sorts of reasons. No one told us about it, for one thing. We did not know there *was* a line until late in the day. But even if we had, we might not have done much about it. We know all kinds of things we do not do much about. There are so many things we mean to do that we never get around to doing, and there are so many things we mean not to do that we end up doing anyway. Even when we manage to do our best, things get in the way: People get sick, businesses fail, relationships go down the drain. There are a lot of reasons why people wind up at the end of the line, and only God can sort them all out.

But suppose for a moment that it is *you* back there, craning your neck for even a glimpse of the theatre, knowing you will never make it, that all the tickets will be gone long before you get there, and that you are about to have one more long, hot afternoon on your hands while everyone else is laughing and eating popcorn inside the cool, dark theatre. It makes you want to cry; it makes you want to give up, when all of a sudden a stir goes through the crowd, the manager appears out of nowhere and walks right up to you, a stack of blue tickets in his hand. "We're starting at this end today," he says, handing you your ticket, and everyone at the end of the line begins to cheer.

God is not fair. For reasons we may never know, God seems to love us indiscriminately, and seems also to enjoy reversing the systems we set up to explain why God should love some of us more than others of us. By starting at the end of our lines, with the last and the least, God lets us know that his ways are not our ways, and that if we want to see things his way we might question our own notions of what is fair, and why we get so upset when our lines do not work.

God is not fair, but depending on where you are in line that can sound like powerful good news, because if God is not fair, then there is a chance we will get paid more than we are worth, that we will get more than we deserve, that we will make it through the doors even though we are last in line—not because of who *we* are but because of who *God* is.

God is not fair; God is *generous*, and when we begrudge that generosity it is only because we have forgotten where we stand. On any given day of our lives, when the sun goes down and a cool breeze stirs the dusk, when the work is done and the steward heads toward the end of the line to hand out the pay, there is a very good chance that the cheers and back slapping, the laughter and gratitude with which he is greeted will turn out to be our own.

15

On the Clouds of Heaven

Matthew 24:29–44

"Immediately after the tribulation of those days the sun will be darkened, and the moon will not give its light, and the stars will fall from heaven, and the powers of the heavens will be shaken; then will appear the sign of the Son of man in heaven, and then all the tribes of the earth will mourn, and they will see the Son of man coming on the clouds of heaven with power and great glory; and he will send out his angels with a loud trumpet call, and they will gather his elect from the four winds, from one end of heaven to the other.

"From the fig tree learn its lesson: as soon as its branch becomes tender and puts forth its leaves, you know that summer is near. So also, when you see all these things, you know that he is near, at the very gates. Truly, I say to you, this generation will not pass away till all these things take place. Heaven and earth will pass away, but my words will not pass away.

"But of that day and hour no one knows, not even the angels of heaven, nor the Son, but the Father only. As were the days of Noah, so will be the coming of the Son of man. For as in those days before the flood they were eating and drinking, marrying and giving in marriage, until the day when Noah entered the ark, and they did not know until the flood came and swept them all away, so will be the coming of the Son of man. Then two men will be in the field; one is taken and one is left. Two women will be grinding at the mill; one is taken and one is left. Watch therefore, for you do not know on what day your Lord is coming. But know this, that if the householder had known in what part of the night the thief was coming, he would have watched and would not have let his house be broken into. Therefore you also must be ready; for the Son of man is coming at an hour you do not expect."

Years and years ago now, way back in the early seventies, I had a vision of the end time. It was probably no coincidence that the world itself was looking pretty terminal at that point. John and Bobby Kennedy had both been buried by then, along with Martin Luther King Jr. Boys I knew were so afraid of being drafted for Vietnam that their hands shook when they dialed the combinations on their mailboxes at the campus post office. Meanwhile, the rest of us were making all the noise we could, taking over administration buildings and marching in the streets. A girl our age had been shot dead by National Guardsmen during a protest at Kent State. We had all seen the picture.

One night in the middle of all this there was a terrific thunderstorm. I lay on the bed in my dorm room watching the sky light up with blast after blast of raw electricity. Even though it was way past midnight, the sky was luminous, with all the night lights of Atlanta hitting the low clouds and thudding back down again. The color was greenish brown—not a right color for the sky to be, which made me feel a little queasy inside.

I could not sleep. I had not slept well in weeks. I did not know what I wanted to be when I grew up. I did not even know if I *wanted* to grow up in such a violent, crazy world. Then I heard myself say, "Come, Lord Jesus"—just like that—and then I said it again: "Come, Lord Jesus." I remember thinking I should be afraid to say something like that, but I wasn't. I was relieved to go ahead and ask for the end. *Please come back and finish this thing up. We are no good at it. We have never been any good at it. Come, Lord Jesus, and don't delay.*

Then I looked out the window and saw (imagined?) a bright spot in the sky that grew bigger and bigger, with clouds boiling all around the center of it like big curling waves. Then the head of a beautiful white horse pushed through them, then the front legs, then the chest, until finally this gleaming creature was galloping right toward me with a rider on its back who was too bright for me to see. There was a lot going on in the background too, like the wake behind a giant speedboat, but I never got a good look at that because I could not take my eyes off the horse and rider.

It only lasted for a second or two. Then I stopped imagining (seeing?) and the thunderstorm moved on. I fell asleep, survived college, grew up, got a job—but that vision of the end remains vivid for me. It is embarrassingly literal, I know. In my part of the country, it might be called a vision of the rapture, and there are plenty of people who would be happy to tell me exactly where it comes in the final lineup of events.

They do not get their information from the Bible, however. Whether they know it or not, they owe most of their eschatology to a renegade Anglican priest from Ireland named John Nelson Darby, who spent a large part of the nineteenth century preaching something called "premillennial dispensationalism." According to Mr. Darby, human history is divided up into seven ages, or "dispensations," all leading up to the end of time. We live under the "dispensation of grace," when people are judged according to their personal relationship with Jesus Christ, but between now and the "dispensation of the millennial kingdom," things are going to get ugly.

There is going to be a Great Tribulation, which those whom Jesus recognizes as his own will not have to endure. God will remove the elect by means of the rapture before judging the earth. Then Israel will be restored as "God's primary instrument in history,"* the wicked will be destroyed in the final battle of Armageddon, and Christ will begin a thousand-year reign on earth.

---

*Donald Wagner, "Evangelicals and Israel: Theological Roots of a Political Alliance," *Christian Century*, November 4, 1998, p. 1020.

Even I, who am not one of Mr. Darby's followers, was surprised to learn that the word "rapture" never occurs in the Bible, but at least one curious side effect of his scenario has been the political alliance between Christian evangelicals in this country and the Likud party in Israel, both of whom—for their own reasons—want to see Israel, not Palestine, in charge of the Holy Land.

The only reason I go over all of this is so that you know where it comes from. It comes from John Darby and his followers, not from Scripture, but since it answers a lot of questions that Scripture won't answer, it is very popular right now, especially among people who do not like surprises. Some of these folks are *informed*. They know who will be saved and who will be lost. They know who the antichrist is and where the Messiah will appear. These are the people who have bumper stickers on their cars that say, "Warning: In case of the rapture, the driver of this car will disappear." Lately I have been seeing some others that say, "When the rapture comes, can I have your car?"

Matthew might not have been quite that flip, but he definitely belonged to the second crowd. He was not concerned with reading signs and keeping timetables, at least partly because he knew how preoccupied people could get with those things. Before long they cared more about their calculations than they did about their neighbors. Once they had figured out who God's 144,000 elect were, they did not waste any time or courtesy on the damned, except perhaps to remind them just how hot hellfire was going to be. Meanwhile, God's chosen had plenty else to do: flee the cities, arm themselves against the enemy, purify themselves for their journey to heaven.

Once they had gotten themselves all worked up about this, Matthew found it just about impossible to impress them with the fact that there were widows and orphans in the community going hungry because no one was signing up for the soup kitchen, or that there were still some people in jail who needed visiting, as well as some sick people at home who still needed looking after. But what did any of that matter, when the end was right around the corner?

Ironically, Matthew had the same problem with those who had *given up* looking for the end. They had stayed pretty focused for the first ten or twenty years, when there were still people around who had actually seen and heard Jesus, but once his disciples began to die off and the eyewitness reports about him became second- or third-hand stories, people's ardor began to cool. If the stories were true, then where was he? If he was so full of love, then why hadn't he come back?

Things had never been worse in Palestine. The chosen people were scattered, the Temple was destroyed, the promised land was a province of Rome, and there was no relief in sight. "Truly, I say to you, this generation will not pass away till all these things take place," Jesus said, but something had obviously gone wrong. Most of the generation that heard him say that *had* passed away, and the ones who were still alive had beards down to their knees. God's alarm clock must not have gone off. Or had God forgot? A third possibility: there never was a God at all.

With questions like that in mind, Matthew made sure to include Jesus' disclaimer that even *he* did not know when the end would come. "No one knows," Jesus said, "not even the angels of heaven, nor the Son, but the Father only" (24:36). That left only one practical alternative, which served as Matthew's bottom line: "Watch therefore, for you do not know on what day your Lord is coming" (24:42). *If Jesus doesn't know when, then you sure don't know when, so why don't you stop obsessing about when and pay attention to what is happening around you right now?*

In a way, the twenty-fourth chapter of Matthew's Gospel reads like a three-act play about the end time. Starting with the first verse, each act lasts about fifteen verses. Each contains a description of events still to come, and each ends with a renewed call to discipleship in the here and now. That makes Matthew a pretty good psychologist as well as an evangelist. He knows that while anxiety and apathy may look like two different disorders, they both respond to the same treatment, which is a focused assignment of some kind. So in each of his acts he describes a virtue that believers may practice whether the sun is falling out of the sky or not.

In act 1, the virtue is enduring love, in act 2 it is discernment, and in act 3 it is alertness, or mindfulness—the moment-by-moment willingness to stay awake to all that is. Any of you who have ever tried to meditate—or even to say the Lord's Prayer all the way through without letting your mind wander off—know how difficult this is. The present moment is just too slippery for most of us to hang on to. As hard as we try, we tend to slide off into what happened yesterday or what we have to do an hour from now, and whether our problem is preoccupation with the future or disillusionment with the past, the end result is that very few of us live our lives while they are actually happening to us. We are cut off from the present. God cannot get to us through all the layers of regret and expectation that we have swaddled ourselves in.

For instance, I am so mired in the past that I almost never meet anyone new. Or more to the point, I rarely give anyone a chance to be new. When someone I do not know walks up to me with a hungry look in her eyes, then I treat her like the last person I met who looked like that. This woman may have an entirely different story. She may be an angel of God sent to tell me something I desperately need to know, but I cannot even see her. All I can see is the last person whom she reminds me of, which means that this new person does not have a chance to get through to me.

I have a similar problem with the future, which is the closet where I store all my good intentions about the people in my life whom I am going to treat better one day real soon. I am not always going to be this busy and unfocused, I tell myself. Any moment now I am going to have time to do the things I have always meant to do and say the things I have always meant to say. I am going to be a better godparent. I am going to pray more. I am going to make my life count. In the meantime, this vision of the future gets me off the hook today. I can even fool myself into believing that my splendid intentions make me a better person right now, and that time will forever expand to meet my needs.

These are my own personal delusions, but they affect communities and nations as well. According to Matthew, it is time to wake up. No matter where Jesus is, it is time to stop living in the past and in the future and to start living right now, because whenever the end comes, that is when it will come—in the now—and meanwhile, our best chance at discovering what abundant life is all about is to start living into it right now, not only one by one but also all together.

I remember something one of my professors told me once, about how the second coming of Christ was an idea cooked up by some church father with only two fingers. The truth, he said, is that Christ comes again, and again, and again—that God has placed no limit on coming to the world, but is always on the way to us here and now. The only thing we are required to do is to notice—to watch, to keep our eyes peeled.

"Therefore you also must be ready, for the Son of man is coming at an hour you do not expect." How do you deal with a piece of advice like that? Well, why not be ready all the time, not only for the end but for whatever the moment brings? Every morning when you wake up, decide to live the life God has given you to live right now. Refuse to live yesterday over and over again. Resist the temptation to save your best self for tomorrow. Do not put off living the kind of life you meant to live.

There is no time for that, no matter how much time is left. Go ahead and make the decision, write the letter, get the help you need, find someone to love, give yourself away. Why waste your time making preparations for an end time you cannot predict? *Live* prepared. Live a caught-up life, not a put-off life, so that wherever you are—standing in a field or grinding at the mill, or just going about the everyday business of your life— you are ready for God, for whatever happens next, not afraid but wide awake, watching for the Lord who never tires of coming to the world.

Who knows? Ours may be the generation that finally sees him ride in on the clouds, or we may meet him the same way generations before us have—one by one by one, as each of us closes our eyes for the last time. Either way, our lives are in God's hands. Either way, God leaves the living of them to us. To God be all honor and glory, now and forever.